# DONALD TRUMP IN 100 FACTS

### RUTH ANN MONTI

AMBERLEY

Dedication

This book practically wrote itself over the last few months of the surreal year
2017. At times, I became so distressed Trump invaded my dreams; and not in
that way! Many days, I still awaken and think, 'how did this happen?' Within
two weeks of submitting the manuscript, I found myself identifying new facts.
It's hard to turn off Trump.

I would be remiss if I didn't thank April Holle, who told me about the
documentary *Meet the Trumps* and reminded me about the horse burgers
(Fact #5). Andrew Lacey, Denise Surk and Lisa Lyons were my steadfast
cheerleaders.

I dedicate this book to my late mother, who would be astonished by this
White House, and my son, who provided an excellent barometer for
determining which facts to include.

Ruth Ann Monti, Scottsdale, AZ

First published 2018

Amberley Publishing
The Hill, Stroud
Gloucestershire, GL5 4EP

www.amberley-books.com

British Library Cataloguing in Publication Data.
A catalogue record for this book is available from the British Library.

ISBN 978 1 4456 7853 5 (paperback)
ISBN 978 1 4456 7854 2 (ebook)

Typeset in 9.5pt on 12.5pt Sabon.
Typesetting and Origination by Amberley Publishing.
Printed in the UK.

# Contents

# 1. DONALD TRUMP IS A MIDDLE CHILD

Donald John Trump was born June 14, 1946, the fourth of five children of Fred Trump Sr and Mary Anne MacLeod Trump. Besides Donald, there is:

Maryanne Trump Barry
Frederick (Freddy) Trump Jr
Elizabeth Trump Grau
Robert Trump

Maryanne Trump Barry (b. 1937) has a long career as a judge. President Ronald Reagan appointed her to the US District Court for the District of New Jersey in 1983. President Bill Clinton elevated her to the US Court of Appeals, Third Circuit, in 2009. She became a senior judge in 2011 and served the court until 2017, when she made her status inactive after Donald became President.

Frederick Trump Jr (1938-1981] suffered from alcoholism. According to an interview Donald gave to the Christian Broadcasting Network, Fred began drinking in college. He was 'a fabulous guy, the best-looking guy, he loved life, he loved people... but he drank a lot.'[1]

Although Fred Sr intended Fred Jr to follow him into the real estate business, the younger Trump lacked his father's drive and according to Donald, 'really didn't love the business and wasn't particularly good at it.' Friends say he was miserable there.[2]

Fred had learned to fly planes while attending Lehigh University in Pennsylvania. He left real estate to work for TWA, married an airline attendant, and had two children. As his alcoholism worsened, he quit flying and was divorced. He moved into his

1 Brody, David. 'The Human Side: Donald Trump Talks About The Death Of His Brother To Alcoholism.' CBN News, 12 July 2015, www1.cbn.com/thebrodyfile/ archive/2015/07/12/the-human-side-donald-trump-talks-about-the-death-of.
2 Kassel, Matthew. 'Why Donald Trump's Brother Robert Has Been Lying Low During This Election.' *Town & Country*, 26 Oct. 2017, www. townandcountrymag.com/society/money-and-power/news/a8479/ robert-trump/.

parents' house and worked on a maintenance crew. He died in 1981 at just 43.

Elizabeth Trump Grau (b. 1942) worked as an administrative assistant for Chase Manhattan Bank for most of her career. She also attended Southern Seminary College, now Southern Virginia University.

In 1989, she married James Walter Grau, president of Charisma Productions, which makes documentaries and sports movies. Trump served as an usher, and older sister Maryanne was matron of honor.

Robert Trump (b. 1948) is two years younger than Donald and the youngest in the family. He worked in the family real estate business his entire life until retiring in 2014.

Like his older brother, Robert was often featured in New York tabloids during the 1980s and 1990s, although he didn't court publicity as actively as Donald. He married a popular socialite, Blaine Beard, in 1984 and divorced in 2008 after he fell in love with his secretary. He bought her a $3.7 million home in Connecticut, where he appears to happily spend most of his time and supports local causes and businesses. 'He's not flamboyant,' one local told *Town & Country*, who described him as classy and dignified. He couldn't be more different than his brother...I don't even know how they're in the same family.'

## 2. TRUMP MAY BE DESCENDED FROM A WEREWOLF OR HIS LOVER

*The Mirror*, a publication at least as reliable as the White House Press Office, reported on October 31, 2107 (Halloween!) that Donald Trump might be descended from Katharina Trump, a woman who may have been the lover of a 16th-century serial killer/cannibal Peter Stumpf, also known as 'The Werewolf of Bedburg.'[1]

Kevin Pittle, PhD, an associate professor in the Department of Anthropology at Biola University in California, came across Katharina. He soon got his colleagues involved with socio-linguistic and ancestral research, and they concluded that Katharina may, in fact, be Donald's ancestor. It's worth noting that the Trump name itself was Anglicized from Drumpf when Trump's grandfather immigrated to America. Drumpf is awfully close to Stumpf. Perhaps Katharina's family changed it to Trump.

Trump would no doubt agree that Peter Stumpf was one bad hombre. He was a farmer convicted of murdering and eating 13 children and two pregnant women. He was also said to have murdered his own son and eaten his brain. Not surprisingly, his story went down as a werewolf tale. To top it off, he was also suspected of incest with his daughter and sister.

The *Mirror* story includes a photo of a pamphlet from the British Library that illustrates the capture of a werewolf (presumably Strumpf), and a man being tried, attached to a Catherine-wheel kind of device, and beheaded. The headless body was then burned at the stake.

It seems 16th-century Germans didn't know werewolves can only be killed with a silver bullet.

---

1 Robson, Steve. 'Strange but true? Donald Trump Could be Related to 16th Century Cannibal Serial Killer 'The Werewolf of Bedburg." *The Mirror*, 31 Oct. 2017, www.mirror.co.uk/news/weird-news/strange-true-donald-trump-could-11415687.

# 3. TRUMP'S MOTHER EMIGRATED FROM SCOTLAND AT EIGHTEEN ON A SHIP CALLED *TRANSYLVANIA*

Trump's mother, Mary Anne MacLeod Trump (1912–2000), was born in a remote fishing village on one of the islands of the Outer Hebrides. She was the youngest of ten children. Her family spoke Scottish Gaelic, and like her siblings, she learned English as a second language at school. The family belonged to the Church of Scotland, and her father worked as a compulsory officer and fisherman.

Mary Anne emigrated in May 1930, one week before her 18th birthday on the RMS *Transylvania* sailing from Glasgow. Although her son has said she came to America on holiday, she had only $50 with her and was listed on the ship's Alien Passenger List as a domestic. (She had also checked 'no' on an immigration form asking if she intended to return to her home country and declared her intention to become a US citizen.) Mary Anne lived with an older sister, Catherine Reid, on Long Island, New York, where she did indeed work as a domestic for about four years. Catherine had left Scotland years earlier to escape the scandal of giving birth out of wedlock.

Mary Anne met her future husband Fred Trump at a dance. Fred was a few years older and already established as builder and developer in Queens, one of the five boroughs that make up New York City. They were married in New York City's Madison Avenue Presbyterian Church in January 1936, whose congregation dates to 1834, making it one of the city's oldest. Its location on Madison Avenue in Manhattan makes it one of the city's tonier churches as well, even back then. Mary Anne and Fred had a small reception of 25 guests at the very elegant Carlyle Hotel.

According to a profile in *The New Yorker*, Mary Anne was just one of many Scottish immigrants who came to New York to escape poverty. In the UK, people from the Hebrides were often looked down upon and most who left were quiet about their Scots Gaelic background. This makes Mary Anne's fortuitous marriage particularly notable.[1] As journalist Torcuil Crichton says in the documentary *Meet the Trumps*, Mary Anne 'went from being a domestic to a domestic goddess.'[2]

She enjoyed the life of a wealthy woman and was often seen in furs and fine jewelry. Like many wealthy New Yorkers, she supported charities, in her case, for people with cerebral palsy and adults with intellectual disabilities.

Although the 1940 US Census lists both Fred and Mary Anne as US citizens, Mary Anne didn't become a 'naturalized' US citizen until 1942. Contrary to some claims, she never resided illegally in the US.

In 1991, Mary Anne was seriously wounded in an attack near her home in Queens, NY and suffered broken ribs, facial injuries, several fractures, a brain hemorrhage, and permanent damage to her eyesight and hearing. She died in 2000 at age 88, just one year after Fred. She is buried alongside her husband and eldest son Freddy Jr.

1 Pilon, Mary. 'Donald Trump's Immigrant Mother.' *The New Yorker*, 19 June 2017, www.newyorker.com/news/news-desk/donald-trumps-immigrant-mother.
2 Berczeller, Paul, and Radice, Mark (Directors). (2017). *Meet the Trumps: From Immigrant to President* [Documentary]. Channel 4 Television Corporation.

## 4. DONALD'S FATHER, FREDERICK CHRIST TRUMP, STARTED OUT BUILDING AFFORDABLE HOUSING

No one has had more influence over Donald Trump than his father Fred, whose drive and ambition he inherited. But unlike his son, Fred built houses and flats priced for middle-income and working class families.

Fred grew up quite comfortable, thanks to the drive of his father, Friedrich (also called Fred), a Bavarian immigrant who came to the US in 1885 at age 16. The elder Fred died when the younger was barely in his teens, but he left his family pretty comfortable thanks to the successful hotels he established in Canada during the Klondike Gold Rush in the late 1800s.

Fred started his own construction business at age 18. He wasn't old enough to sign bank checks, so he partnered with his mother Elizabeth (née Christ) and named the business E. Trump & Son. (The name lasted until Donald took over the business decades later.) With an $800 loan from Elizabeth, Fred built his first single-family home in Queens, New York, in 1923 and sold it for $7600. He went on to build other modest single-family homes and later built multi-family flats as well.

Construction halted when the Great Depression hit the US in 1929. Fred built a self-service market and called it Trump Market. He sold it after six months to a supermarket chain. It must have been traumatic to see his name torn down because he swore he would never again put the Trump name on a building.

During the war, E. Trump & Son took advantage of US Government funds to build houses for returning soldiers and their families. In *Meet the Trumps*, journalists Wayne Barrett and Gwenda Blair noted the irony that a New Deal program was Fred's big break. 'He was first in line in the New York regional office' to apply for funds, Blair remarked.[1]

In 1964, Fred undertook his most ambitious project to date, Trump Village, a seven-building, $70 million complex of flats in

---

1 *Meet the Trumps*, 2017.

Coney Island in Brooklyn. ('It took a long time to sell me on the idea' of putting his name on the complex, he told a reporter.)

In all, he built 27,000 flats for middle and lower-income New York City residents, almost all in the 'outer boroughs' of Brooklyn and Queens. One paper called him 'the Henry Ford of the Home-Building Industry.'[2]

Although he became a millionaire, Fred continued to live in the rather majestic home in Queens he built in the 1950s. Donald says he was very frugal and would often be seen picking up nails and other debris at construction sites that might be usable elsewhere. (You could say he was an early recycler.) He even mixed his own cleaning solutions for buildings where his company provided janitorial services.

Fred Trump suffered from Alzheimer's for several years before he died from pneumonia in 1999. He was buried near his son Freddy Jr. Donald keeps a framed photo of him on a table behind his desk in the Oval Office.

---

2 Clipping from *The Bridgeport Post*. Newspapers.com, UPI, https://goo.gl/ADfgCv.

# 5. TRUMP'S PATERNAL GRANDFATHER LEFT GERMANY ILLEGALLY AND MADE HIS FORTUNE IN CANADA

Fred's father Friedrich came to the US in 1885 as a 16-year old immigrant from Kallstadt, Bavaria, now the German state of Rhineland-Palatinate. He did not tell the authorities he planned to emigrate, which came back to haunt him years later.

Friedrich found work as a hairdresser—he'd been a barber's apprentice in Germany—and became a US citizen in 1892. Two years later, he moved to Seattle, a young city deeply involved in the lumber industry. He opened two restaurants there and sold them in 1897 to head for the Klondike Gold Rush. His timing was perfect; within a couple of years, Seattle was engulfed in a fire that destroyed much of its downtown area.

Friedrich was quite the adventurer. He took a boat to Alaska and hiked with his supplies over to Canada's Yukon Territory. He built a boat to get over the Yukon River to reach the White Pass route to the gold mines. Along the way, he collected carcasses of horses that had died en route and opened a canteen where he sold horse burgers. Later, he opened a hotel where, as Gwenda Blair notes in her book *The Trumps: Three Generations That Built an Empire*, Friedrich 'mined the miners' who took the opportunity to rest and eat for a few days.[1]

This turned out to be an excellent business model. Friedrich went on to open the Arctic Hotel and Restaurant in British Columbia. As business started to dwindle, he decided to relocate down the river to Whitehorse. In *Meet the Trumps*, historian Wayne Barrett describes how Fred took the hotel apart and tried to float it down the river. When it fell apart, he dragged what he could ashore and rebuilt it in the middle of Whitehorse—on a lot he didn't own but refused to vacate.[2]

The hotel was quite popular for its excellent menu—fresh fish, caribou, duck, local berries, and alcohol. It also attracted illegal

1 Blair, Gwenda, *The Trumps: Three Generations That Built an Empire*. Simon & Schuster, 2000.

2 *Meet the Trumps*, 2017.

gambling, prostitutes, and lots of eager miners, Blair writes. A local newspaper recommended it for 'single men' but not 'respectable women.'[2]

To be fair, prostitution was common during the many Gold Rushes that struck the North American continent. Few people would blame Friedrich if he created his own art of a deal to get a (financial) piece of the action. But in 1900, the Canadian Royal Mounties announced a crackdown on prostitution and out-of-control drinking. Rather than stick it out, Friedrich wisely sold his assets in 1901 before the boom imploded. He returned to Germany with a small fortune and married Elisabeth Christ in 1902.

Friedrich learned that he lost his German citizenship by leaving and not returning to fulfill mandatory military service. That's when things got bumpy, according to an interview with a local historian in the German paper *Bild*. He wrote to local authorities asking them to reinstate his citizenship, which was not only denied, but came with an order to leave within eight weeks or face deportation. He sent several letters pleading with Bavaria's Prince Luitpold who ruled over the local council. He was given an additional two months before he was forced to leave.

Back in America, Friedrich worked as a hotel manager in Manhattan and invested in Queens real estate. He kept a low profile, though, as the First World War broke out and anti-German sentiment emerged. He died a victim of the 1918 flu pandemic that killed millions around the world, leaving behind a nice nest egg for his wife and children worth that would be worth about half a million dollars today.

# 6. AS A CHILD, TRUMP WAS A TROUBLEMAKER INSIDE AND OUTSIDE SCHOOL

'Little Donny was a lot like candidate Donald Trump,' *The Washington Post* observed in a 2016 article that included interviews with people who grew up with Trump.[1]

'When I look at myself in the first grade and I look at myself now, I'm basically the same person,' Trump told biographer Michael D'Antonio.[2]

In spite of growing up in a rather strict home, few people from Trump's childhood recall him as being hampered by rules. He threw things—board erasers at school, cake at parties. A younger neighbor, now a physician, recalls his mother talking about the time she caught Donald throwing rocks over a fence at him 'for target practice.' At the time, the future physician was still in a playpen.

While his parents forbade cursing or even nicknames, other neighbors remember hearing Donald and friends 'shout and curse very loudly' as they rode their bicycles around the neighborhood. The physician remembers them chasing down a lone boy to beat him up. 'He was a loudmouth bully,' the physician says. '[The beating is] kind of like a little video snippet that remains in my brain because I think it was so unusual and terrifying at that age.'[1]

In fact, no one seems to remember young Trump with much fondness. Descriptions range from 'bully' to 'mischievous' to 'surly,' the last from a teacher at the Kew-Forest School he attended in Queens and where he was punished with after-school detention so often his initials became local shorthand for it.

Kew-Forest, founded in 1918, is the oldest independent (e.g., private) school in Queens. According to its website, it seeks to 'foster a lifelong love of learning.' It didn't work with young Donald, whose behavior stressed out pretty much everyone he encountered. He disrupted classes, threw blackboard erasers at

---

1 Schwartzman, Paul, and Michael E. Miller. 'Confident. Incorrigible. Bully: Little Donny Was a Lot like Candidate Donald Trump.' *The Washington Post*, 22 June 2016, goo.gl/M71jwH.

2 D'Antonio, Michael. *Never Enough: Donald Trump and the Pursuit of Success*. (Thomas Dunne Books, 2015).

teachers, talked out of turn (no surprise to anyone who watched any of the Presidential debates), taunted other children, and for years bragged that he punched a music teacher (not true, according to the teacher's family), all the earmarks of a bully.

One classmate did fight back, hitting Trump on the head with her metal lunchbox after he'd pulled her hair in class. It remains her only memory of him. 'I must have been quite annoyed,' she told *The Post*.

Charles Walker, the teacher Trump said he punched, learned on his deathbed in 2015 that Trump was considering a bid for the Presidency. 'When that kid was 10,' he told the family gathered around, 'even then he was a little s—t.'[1]

Trump's father, biographer Michael D'Antonio says, was nevertheless kind of impressed with his rebellious middle child, who he thought was most like himself. Still, he wasn't happy with reports he was getting from school. Once he learned that Donald and a friend had been sneaking into Manhattan to buy switchblades—the gangs depicted in the play *West Side Story* impressed them—Dad had had enough. He picked up the phone and called the New York Military Academy.

# 7. TRUMP'S FATHER SENT HIM TO MILITARY SCHOOL TO STRAIGHTEN UP AND FLY RIGHT

Trump was sent to the New York Military Academy (NYMA), a private military school at age 13 because he parents thought he would benefit from the discipline there. It was probably a huge relief for the staff at Kew-Forest!

Donald was caught completely off-guard by this development. He went from a luxurious home with a cook, chauffeur, and 'the most amazing train set' to a place best known for straightening out troubled boys. He was required to make his bed, shine his shoes, clean his sink, and do his homework. Cadets were not permitted off-campus during the week, and wore whatever they were told for different activities.

In an interview with *The Washington Post*, Trump's mentor, US Army Colonel Theodore Dobias, said that even after Donald adjusted to the routines, there were still glimpses of the Once and Future Donald. 'He wanted to be number one. He wanted to be noticed. He wanted to be recognized. And he liked compliments,' Colonel Dobias says.[1] It helped that he was a standout baseball player, which gave him some of the recognition he craved.

Over time, Trump enthusiastically embraced the school's pomp and circumstance. 'I did very well under the military system and became one of the top guys at the whole school,' Trump told *Post* reporter Michael E. Miller. He was voted 'Ladies Man' in his senior year yearbook in 1964, posing with a young woman who, it turns out, worked as a secretary at the school and was married to one of the teachers.

But it wouldn't be Trump if there weren't a controversy. Early in his last year at the school, Trump was named a captain, a big honor that includes commanding lower-ranking student officers. But a month later, he was transferred to a new job with the school staff that had no command responsibilities. This job had its perks; he moved out of the barracks and into an administration building.

1 Schwartzman and Miller, 'Confident. Incorrigible. Bully.' *The Washington Post*, 2016.

According to Trump, it was a reward and promotion for his stellar performance. Others remember things differently.

Former cadets told *The Post* that the switch came after school officials received hazing complaints about lower-ranking officers under his command. They concluded that Trump spent too much time in his room rather than actually commanding underclassmen.[2] As a private school, NYMA graduates are not required to serve in the military and few actually do. Trump has often said he learned as much as 'the generals' at NYMA.

NYMA has suffered financially for many years. In 2011, administrators appealed to Trump for a donation, which *Business Insider* reports he declined to give.[3] The school filed for bankruptcy in 2015 and was sold at auction to a nonprofit conservation group owned by Chinese real estate billionaire Vincent Tianquan Mo.

2 Miller, Michael E. '50 Years Later, Disagreements over Young Trump's Military Academy Record.' *The Washington Post*, 9 Jan. 2016, https://goo.gl/g1Khqf.
3 Robinson, Melia. 'Trump Says This Private Boarding School Gave Him More Military Training than the Army Could – Take a Look.' *Business Insider*, 15 Dec. 2016, goo.gl/ABGGWU.

# 8. FREDDY TRUMP JR PROVIDED A CAUTIONARY TALE TO DONALD

Trump has said several times that his older brother Freddy's alcoholism left a huge impression on him. He says Freddy himself warned him to stay away from alcohol and cigarettes, and seeing the toll they took on him, this wasn't difficult. 'I've never drank and I've never smoked,' Donald told the Christian Broadcast Network, adding that he has told all his children the same from the time they were still very young.[1]

Although raised Episcopalian, Freddy joined a Jewish fraternity at Lehigh University, possibly to annoy his father. His fraternity brothers loved his middle name—Christ—and Freddy enjoyed the joke as much as they. It actually took everyone a while to realize that the generous, fun-loving, Corvette-driving student was quite wealthy. Later, he took friends out on his speedboat, often picking up his 'pain-in-the-ass-brother' to take along.[2]

Although Freddy was eight years older, Donald often scolded him for lacking the drive he shared with their father. A friend of Freddy's recalled a dinner in the mid-1960s when Trump, still in college, joined them for the meal and ended up berating Freddy to 'grow up, get serious, and make something of yourself.' Donald 'put Freddy down quite a bit,' the friend said. 'There was a lot of combustion.'[2]

Fred Sr was no less tough on all his children, unfortunately, his eldest 'wasn't a killer,' Donald said. Moreover, Fred Jr didn't defend himself, an error Donald learned from and took to heart.[3] Fred 'struggled to fit in' with the Trump organization, Trump biographer Michael D'Antonio said in a video produced by *Business Insider*.[4] He left real estate and followed his dream

1  David Brody, 'The Human Side.' CBN, 2015.
2  Horowitz, Jason. 'For Donald Trump, Lessons From a Brother's Suffering.' *The New York Times*, 2 Jan. 2016, https://goo.gl/v1NTrM.
3  Blair, Gwenda. *Donald Trump: Master Apprentice*. (Simon & Schuster, 2005).
4  *The tragic story of Donald Trump's late brother Fred*. Produced by Joe Avella, video interview with Michael D'Antonio, *Business Insider*, 12 Feb. 2016, http://www.businessinsider.com/donald-trumps-brother-fred-trump-jr-2016-2.

to become a pilot. He obtained a commercial pilot's license and got a job flying with TransWorld Airlines, where he also met and married a flight attendant.

Part of the story, D'Antonio says, is that Donald joked that 'pilots are essentially bus drivers in the sky,' something he feels Fred probably didn't see as a joke but as belittling. As a result, they probably weren't very close, 'although Donald says he mourns his brother.'[4] Trump has, in fact, spoken fondly of Fred in interviews and speeches, including his Presidential victory speech and later in an October 2016 address on responding to the opioid crisis in the US.

Fred's drinking continued and he voluntarily quit TWA lest he become a danger to passengers. He tried his hand as a fishing boat captain in Florida, a venture that ultimately failed.

Freddy stood as Donald's best man at his 1977 wedding to Ivanka, something Donald hoped would encourage him. But Fred's drinking continued, and he died four years later from a massive heart attack, not an unusual fate for alcoholics.

'He would have been an amazing peacemaker if he didn't have [a drinking] problem,' Trump has said. 'Everybody loved him. He's like the opposite of me.'[2]

# 9. MOST OF TRUMP'S UNIVERSITY CLASSMATES DON'T REMEMBER HIM

Trump graduated from The Wharton School of Business at The University of Pennsylvania, an Ivy League school considered one of the nation's best. He had transferred there after two years at Fordham University in Bronx, New York. He often highlights his Wharton degree as proof of his brilliance, but the record shows he was an average student. And while Wharton is a fine school, its MBA program, not its undergraduate degree, has built its reputation.

In her book on three generations of Trumps, Gwenda Blair maintains that Trump's older brother Freddy facilitated Trump's transfer to Wharton through his friendship with the school's admissions officer.[1]

Various media, including student journalists at Penn's own newspaper *The Daily Pennsylvanian*, contacted members of the Class of 1968 and found that few remembered him at all. He wasn't on the Dean's List and didn't graduate with any special honors, in spite of a few news articles from the 1970s that said he graduated first in his class (he never contacted those writers to complain about 'fake news').

*The DP* did uncover these remembrances:

Trump 'sat in the front row [of the real estate class], raised his hand a lot to answer questions, and had a heavy New York accent.' At least the New York Military Academy did improve his behavior since his days at Kew-Forest.

He was 'very focused on his studies' and 'professional.'

'Don…was loath to really study much' and often came to study groups unprepared.

He 'spent all his weekends in New York because residential real estate [his focus of study] is a weekend business.'

'He was not an intellectual man but that wasn't what his goal was…he's not an intellectual now, that's pretty obvious.'[2]

1 Gwenda Blair, *Three Generations of Trumps*, 2000.
2 Rabin, Alex, and Tan, Rebecca. 'Was Trump Really a Top Student at Wharton? His Classmates Say Not so Much.' *The Daily Pennsylvanian*, 15 Feb. 2017, www.thedp.com/article/2017/02/trump-academics-at-wharton.

Trump built up the ladies' man reputation he developed at the New York Military Academy at Penn. A classmate remembers he always had 'a pretty girl on his arm'. For at least one night, the actress Candice Bergen was one of them. They had a blind date for which she remembers a lot of burgundy: 'burgundy suit...burgundy boots...burgundy limousine...he was very coordinated.' Trump remembers she was 'dating guys from Paris who were 35 years old...I did not make the move.'[3]

Trump apparently didn't make a lot of connections at Wharton. He lived off-campus and didn't spend weekends there. He apparently pledged a lot of money to Wharton and Penn over the years—another DP article uncovered pledges totalling more than $1.4 billion—but the amount he's actually donated is unknown.[4] Trump is known for pledging donations but rarely following through, as discussed in Facts #36 and 37.

Trump is listed as a founder of the Penn Club in New York, which required a $5,000 donation. His first major donation to the school came in 1996, when he gave the club somewhere between $100,000 and $150,000. This also coincides with Donald Trump Jr's commencement at Penn; Ivanka entered the school in 2000.[4]

---

3  Kranish, Michael and Fischer, Marc. *Trump Revealed*. Scribner, 2016.
4  Sadurni, Luis Ferre. 'Donald Trump May Have Donated over $1.4 Million to Penn.' *The Daily Pennsylvanian*, 3 Nov. 2016, www.thedp.com/article/2016/11/trumps-history-of-donating-to-penn.

## 10. DONALD TRUMP DID NOT SERVE IN THE MILITARY AND USED ALL DEFERMENTS NECESSARY TO AVOID IT

It isn't exactly a secret that Donald Trump didn't serve in the military in spite of attending a military college prep school. He came of age during the Vietnam War when many young men looked for ways to defer their military service or took positions outside the combat zone, even as they went on to become hawkish politicians eager to commit American troops around the world.

Going to university was the most popular way to avoid the Vietnam draft, but many college graduates entered the military after graduation. Graduate school was another way to put more space in front of getting drafted, but the US government eliminated it in 1968 after it realized universities were overflowing with PhD candidates like Republican Party standouts Newt Gingrich, PhD and Dick Cheney, PhD. Other young men looked for some kind of physical ailment that would make them ineligible.

Donald Trump did both. He received a total of five deferments to avoid serving in the Vietnam War draft. The first four were for attending university, first at Fordham University in New York's Bronx borough and later, the University of Pennsylvania. He graduated in 1968, at the height of the Vietnam War.

Trump could have entered the National Guard, state militia that normally remain in their states but have been called up for almost every military action. Many young men joined the Guard hoping they would remain stateside. Despite his proclaimed enjoyment of and success with the military routine, Trump stayed away from the National Guard. Other options included getting married and fathering a child or taking a public service job like teaching. Real estate development, however, was not considered public service.

After graduation, Trump reported for the physical examination that determined a young man's fitness to serve in the military. He took two exams and passed both. He then presented a letter from his physician explaining that he had bone spurs in both heels. It's a little surprising to read this since he played squash, tennis, and golf. But the letter was enough to persuade the local draft board to give him a 1-Y deferment. This would keep him from being drafted except in times of war or national emergency. The US had never actually declared war on North Vietnam; its presence there was classified as a 'police action'.

Trump also drew a high number for the 1969 draft, which made it quite unlikely that he would be drafted that year anyway. And while 1-Y deferments were intended to be temporary, in practice, they lasted as long as one usually needed. In 1972, the last year for which Trump was eligible for the draft, he was classified as 4F, which replaced the 1-Y classification.

Trump could have volunteered to join the fight against the Viet Cong at any time but chose not to. He later joked during the 2016 campaign that his 'personal Vietnam' was 'avoiding venereal disease.'[1]

1 Marquina, Sierra. 'Donald Trump Calls Sleeping Around, Avoiding STDs, His "Personal Vietnam."' 2 Aug. 2016, www.usmagazine.com/celebrity-news/news/donald-trump-calls-sleeping-around-as-his-personal-vietnam-w432176/.

# 11. TRUMP HAS BEEN MARRIED MORE THAN ANY OTHER PRESIDENT BUT STARTED AS A SECOND HUSBAND

Trump has been married more times than any other President and is only the second President to have been divorced (the other is Ronald Reagan).

Trump's first marriage to Ivana Zelnickova lasted from 1977 to 1992. Ivana is a Czech-born Canadian model who says she was an alternate on Czechoslovakia's ski team during the 1972 Olympics (there is some dispute over this). Trump was the second of her four husbands; her first husband was an Austrian skier.

Ivana met Donald in 1972 at a New York City restaurant, Maxwell's Plum. She was in town for a fashion show. He procured a table for Ivana and her friends. 'He said, "I'm Donald Trump and I see you're looking for a table. I can help you,"' Ivana told the *New York Post*. 'I looked at my friends and said, "the good news is, we're getting a table real fast. The bad news is, this guy is going to be sitting with us."' But when Donald paid the bill and disappeared, she was impressed. 'There's something strange because I've never met a man who didn't want anything from a woman and paid for it.' When she walked outside, Donald's limousine was there waiting to take her home.[1]

They began dating and Donald and Ivana went to Aspen, Colorado, to go skiing. Donald didn't know Ivana was a skilled skier. She sat out the first day while he took a lesson on the bunny hill. The second day, she joined him and when he saw her in action, became quite angry. 'I will never [ski] again for anybody,' she recalled him yelling.[1]

They married anyway within the year and had three children between 1977 and 1984, Donald Jr, Ivanka, and Eric. The children were all under 12 by the time the divorce was finalized, with custody going to Ivana.

---

1 Schuster, Dana. 'Ivana Trump on How She Advises Donald - and Those Hands.' *New York Post*, 4 Apr. 2016, https://goo.gl/xu2Gz3.

Ivana became the CEO for the Trump's Castle Casino in Atlantic City, New Jersey, commuting by helicopter. Later, when Trump bought the Plaza Hotel in New York City, he named her its president, telling the media her salary was '1 dollar a year and all the dresses she can buy.'[1]

During their divorce proceedings in 1992, Ivana claimed that Donald violently assaulted her in 1989 after he had botched scalp reduction surgery to remove a bald spot. Ivana had recommended the plastic surgeon. She later toned down the accusation, saying it was 'lawyer's talk' and that she was never abused.[1]

Ivana's divorce settlement included:

$14 million cash
The family's 45-room mansion in Greenwich, Connecticut
An apartment at Trump Plaza in Manhattan
Use of Donald's Mar-a-Lago resort in Palm Beach, Florida every March

Ivana says she is friendly with the current Mrs Trump, Melania, but has no love for Donald's second wife Marla Maples. Maples' appearance at a family ski vacation in Aspen in 1989 led to the Trumps' separation and divorce. Newspapers widely reported that Ivana chased Marla Maples out of a restaurant, shouting 'you bitch, leave my husband alone!'[2]

2  Farrell, Mary H.J. 'Cover Story: The Trumps Head for Divorce Court.' *People*, 26 Feb. 1990, https://goo.gl/y76KrF.

## 12. TRUMP'S AFFAIR WITH MARLA MAPLES WENT ON FOR A COUPLE OF YEARS BEFORE IVANA COULD NO LONGER IGNORE IT

Marla Maples arrived in New York in 1985, not long after she finished as a runner-up in the Miss Hawaiian Tropic International beauty pageant sponsored by the tanning lotion of the same name. A native of Georgia, Maples aspired to be an actress and enrolled in New York's HB studio, which trained stars like Al Pacino, Barbara Streisand, Robert DeNiro, and Anne Bancroft. She ran into one of the Hawaiian Tropic judges, who introduced her to Donald Trump at his office, where she admired the view. They bumped into one another a few more times, including at a charity event and tennis tournament.

Two years later, Marla's agent persuaded her to go to a book party for *The Art of the Deal*, where he thought she could make some connections. The party was at the famous Rainbow Room at Rockefeller Center and was filled with celebrities and politicians. After the event, Trump's longtime assistant Norma Foerderer called Maples to tell her Donald wanted to meet for lunch. She refused, but the calls kept coming. Finally, she accepted.

Maples says she made it clear to Trump over a five-hour lunch that she would not get involved with a married man with children. He told her a divorce from Ivana was inevitable. Trump was already rumored to be seeing other women, and it's likely that Marla was just one of them at first.

In 1989, Rupert Murdoch's New York tabloid, the *Daily News*, ran a photo of Marla on its Page Six gossip sheet. By then, her relationship with Trump was pretty well known. Ivana's friends tried to tell her about Marla, but she brushed them off, opting for extensive plastic surgery to recapture the youth Donald hankered for.

Trump meanwhile was keeping Marla in various Trump properties, including Atlantic City, where Ivana was president of the Trump Castle casino. Things got really ugly when Donald decided to bring Marla along on a family ski vacation in 1989.

Ivana says that was when she first heard of Marla at all; she overheard him on the phone talking about Marla. 'I never heard a name like that in my life,' she reportedly told Donald. 'Who is Moola?' He answered that she was a girl who had been chasing him for the past two years.[1]

Later, at a restaurant, Ivana spotted someone identified as a friend of Marla's. She went up to the woman to tell her to give Marla a message: 'I love my husband very much.'[1] Marla was standing right there as well, but Ivana was unaware. Marla then chose to make herself known and in front of the Trump children, announced her love for Donald. The rest became tabloid history.

Marla went underground for a while, taking a Peace Corps gig in Guatemala while the divorce played out. By 1991, she and Donald were publicly dating and he gave her a 7.5-carat diamond ring—which he said was not meant to be taken as an engagement ring.

---

1  Kranish and Fischer, *Trump Revealed*, 2016.

# 13. TRUMP'S SECOND WIFE, MARLA MAPLES, LEFT NEW YORK TO RAISE THEIR DAUGHTER ALONE

Trump married his second wife, Marla Maples, in December 1993, a couple of months after their daughter Tiffany was born.

The marriage lasted just a few years. They announced their separation in 1997, but according to *The New York Daily News*, they had been living separately for a year and a half and appeared together only for certain social functions. Friends say each was frustrated by the other's career: Marla disliked Trump's fascination with tabloids, while he resented her acting ambitions.[1] While married to Donald, Marla landed roles in local New York theatre and in a few films.

Marla reluctantly settled for $2 million to end the marriage in 1999.[2] Donald moved out just in time to avoid paying a higher settlement as spelt out in their prenuptial agreement. She had also been worn out by lawsuits involving her former agent, who was convicted of burglarizing her apartment the year before she married Donald, and subsequently countersued her and Donald.

Marla moved to California with Tiffany to raise her alone and 'away from the spotlight' and resume her acting career, apparently with Donald's approval. Trump 'loves his kids,' Marla told *People* in 2016, 'and is a good provider with education and such…but everything was a bit of a negotiation.'[2]

Marla never remarried, reluctant to take anything away from her relationship with Tiffany. She encouraged her to maintain a relationship with her father and took her to New York a few times each year to visit her father 'to create some consistency where she could see him.'[2]

---

1 'Donald Trump and Marla Maples Announce Their Separation in 1997.' *NY Daily News*, 2 May 2016, https://goo.gl/vKSTvb.

2 Triggs, Charlotte. 'Donald Trump Ex Marla Maples Talks Raising Tiffany Trump as a Single Mother.' *People*, 21 Apr. 2016, https://goo.gl/XqNB6S.

# 14. MELANIA TRUMP IS THE SECOND FIRST LADY TO BE BORN OUTSIDE THE US AND THE FIRST FROM A COMMUNIST COUNTRY

Slovenian-born Melanie Trump is just the second First Lady to be born outside the US. The last one was Louisa Adams, wife of the sixth President, John Quincy Adams, who was born in London in 1775. She is the first First Lady to have been born and raised in a Communist country as well, and almost certainly speaks more foreign languages than any other First Lady: English, French, Italian, German, Serbo-Croatian, and Slovene.

Melania was born in Novo Mesto, Slovenia, in what was then Yugoslavia. Her father managed car and motorcycle dealerships and her mother worked for a children's clothing manufacturer.

She started modeling as a child and did her first commercial at age 16. She attended the University of Ljubljana for a year and dropped out to pursue a modeling career, signing with an Italian agency that got her jobs with fashion houses in Paris and Milan.

She met Paolo Zamparelli, a friend of Trump's and co-owner of a US modeling agency on one of his scouting trips. He arranged for her to travel to New York where, according to the Associated Press, she worked on 10 jobs and earned about $20,000 before she had legal permission to actually work in the US.[1]

Although she wasn't a top-tier model, she landed some nice gigs and was on the covers of *Harper's Bazaar* (Bulgaria), *Vanity Fair* (Italy), *InStyle*, and *New York Magazine*. She modelled for the Bergdorf Goodman's swimsuit and lingerie catalogs. She posed nude for *GQ* (Great Britain) in 2000 and appeared in the very popular *Sports Illustrated Swimsuit Issue* in the US. She was featured on a billboard in Times Square in New York, for Camel cigarettes and appeared in a commercial for the US insurance company, Aflac, known for its comic adverts and 'spokes duck.'

---

1  Alicia A. Caldwell, Chad Day and Jake Pearson. 'Melania Trump Modeled in US Prior to Getting Work Visa.' Associated Press, 5 Nov. 2016, apnews.com/37dc7aef0ce44077930b7436be7bfd0d.

Melania met Trump during New York Fashion Week 1998, a year after he separated from Marla Maples. Donald approached her for her number, and she insisted on taking his instead. They soon began dating, and Donald moved her parents Viktor and Amalija Knavs to New York. Her old friend Zamparelli insisted in several interviews that Donald is the only man she dated in New York. She was focused on her career and didn't bother with clubs or bars, instead working out at the gym and going to movies by herself. That changed, of course, after she started dating Donald, but like him, she doesn't drink alcohol.

Melania and Donald married after six years of dating. She became pregnant with their son Barron six months after the wedding. According to *Vanity Fair*, Melania promised Donald that she would get her body back after the baby was born.[2]

2 Peretz, Evgenia. 'Inside the Trump Marriage: Melania's Burden.' *Vanity Fair*, 25 May 2017, www.vanityfair.com/news/2017/04/donald-melania-trump-marriage.

# 15. TRUMP IS THE ONLY PRESIDENT TO HAVE CHILDREN WITH THREE DIFFERENT WIVES

Other Presidents have had larger families than Trump's, but none have kids from three different wives.

Trump's three oldest children are from his marriage to Ivana: Donald Jr (born 1977), Ivanka (born 1981), and Eric (born 1984). His daughter Tiffany was born to Marla Maples in 1993, and Barron was born in 2006, a year after he married Melania.

During one of the Town Hall-style Presidential debates, an audience member asked the candidates to say something nice about each other. Hillary Clinton's answer was 'I respect his children. His children are incredibly able and devoted and I think that says a lot about Donald.'[1] It's likely that Clinton has at least met Ivanka Trump a few times as she is close to Clinton's daughter Chelsea.

And while prenuptial agreements forbid Ivana and Marla from saying negative things about Donald, they have said over and over again that he cares deeply about their children. For one thing, they took to heart their father's warnings about drink and drugs. As Donald told the Christian Broadcasting Network: 'From the time they were old enough to listen to me and speak, from a very young age, I used to say "No drinking at all. No drugs, no smoking." I even used to say no coffee! And now I add no tattoos...Literally, like once a week I'd say it.'[2]

Trump's three oldest children have worked closely with him for their entire adult lives. While Donald and Ivana apparently relied on nannies and Ivana's parents for a lot of the children's upbringing, they are pretty well suited for business, if not their performances in the public eye.

1 'What does Clinton respect about Trump? His Kids.' YouTube, uploaded by *PBS News Hour*, 9 Oct. 2016, https://www.youtube.com/watch?v=oaikpEImfTc
2 David Brody, *The Human Side*, CBN, 2015.

## 16. OTHER TRUMP RELATIVES INCLUDE A DECORATED ENGINEER, A KETCHUP MAGNATE, AND A HIGH-RANKING JUDGE

Donald Trump is very, very successful. Other Trump relatives have done well, too.

Trump's uncle John George Trump (1907–1985) was an engineer who developed medical equipment to treat cancer patients. He created rotational radiation therapy, which focuses radiation beams on a tumor from different angles and reduces the amount of time a patient spends in treatment. Later, he helped develop an early million-volt x-ray generator. He received the National Medal of Science from President Ronald Reagan.

Trump's paternal grandfather Friedrich Trump was a second cousin of Henry J. Heinz, who founded H.J. Heinz and popularized catsup as 'ketchup.' Both families hailed from Bavaria.

Heinz's grandson H John Heinz III served in the US House of Representatives in the early 1970s and was later elected to the Senate in 1976. He was re-elected two more times and made a name for himself as a moderate and well-liked Republican. He was killed in 1991 when the helicopter he was riding in collided with another. Six other people died, including two on the ground.

Heinz's widow Teresa later married his Senate colleague John Kerry, who was the Democratic nominee for President in 2004, losing to George W Bush. Kerry later served as Barack Obama's Secretary of State.

Donald's older sister Maryanne Trump Barry helped break a lot of barriers for women in the law profession. She graduated from law school in 1974 at age 37 to launch a career after raising her son. After graduation, she went to work as an Assistant US Attorney for the District of New Jersey to represent the US government in court cases—a little surprising for the daughter and eldest child of a millionaire builder. She went on to leadership positions there before she was named to a federal judgeship in 1983.

In 1999, she was elevated to the US Court of Appeals, a highly influential position. She received a top award for excellence in law and public service given by then-Supreme Court Justice Sandra Day O'Connor, the first woman to serve on the US Supreme Court.

In 2014, German filmmaker Simone Wendel released a documentary, *Kings of Kallstadt*, about the ancestral village where the Trump and Heinz families come from and where she happened to grow up as well. She interviewed various Trump and Heinz relatives as well as Trump himself, who appears in segments with Wendel and his cousin John Walter, a Trump Organization employee who also serves as family historian. 'Ich bin ein Kallstadter,' Trump says in a preview you can see on YouTube.

Wendel brought with her a busload of Kallstadt villagers who were invited to march in New York's Steuben parade, for which Trump was Grand Marshall in 1999. Back home, they discuss what would have become of the Trumps if Friedrich had been permitted to remain in Germany. 'Maybe a vinter,' one woman suggests in a scene at the village's annual wine festival. 'And probably a not-too-shabby one, at that.'[1]

---

1 *Kings of Kallstadt.* Directed by Simone Wendel, 2014.

# 17. A FEUD WITH FRED TRUMP III LED DONALD TO CUT OFF MEDICAL SUPPORT FOR A SICK GREAT-NEPHEW

Donald cut off medical coverage for a great-nephew born with infantile spasms, a rare and dangerous disorder, after the child's father, Fred Trump III and his sister Mary sued him after discovering that they had been cut out of their grandfather's will. The two adult children of Fred Trump Jr claimed Donald influenced Fred Sr, who had Alzheimer's, into altering his will, believed to be about $200 million.[1]

Unaware of the will's contents, Fred III spoke at his grandfather's funeral in June 1999, just two days before his wife went into labor with the third child, a son who required 24-hour care and was later diagnosed with cerebral palsy.

Why seek revenge through a very sick baby, whose life depends on access to medical care? 'I was angry because they sued,' Donald told *The New York Times* in a 2016 interview.[1] By that time, the baby required around the clock nursing and had twice stopped breathing.

Fred III, who received a letter on March 30, 2000 announcing the end of his family's medical benefits, got a judge to reinstate them. 'These are not warm and fuzzy people,' he told the judge. 'They never even came to see William [the baby]. Our family puts the "fun" in dysfunctional.' Asked by the judge if he thought cutting off William's medical coverage was cold-hearted, Uncle Donald responded, 'I can't help that. It's cold when someone sues my father.'[2]

The lawsuit was later settled 'amicably', according to the future president.[1] Fred III works in real estate, but not for Trump.

---

1 Jason Horowitz, 'Lessons From a Brother's Suffering.' *The New York Times*, 2016.

2 Evans, Heidi. 'Inside Trumps' Bitter Battle Nephew's Ailing Baby Caught in the Middle.' *NY Daily News*, 19 Dec. 2000, https://goo.gl/DjWyvv.

# 18. TRUMP'S OBSESSION WITH MODELS, HOLLYWOOD, AND REAL ESTATE MAY HAVE DRIVEN HIS OLDER CHILDREN'S CHOICE OF MARRIAGE PARTNERS

As everyone knows, Trump has been very, very successful in the real estate and entertainment businesses. Marrying a model was in many ways the cherry on the cake and certainly enhanced his already healthy self-image.

Two of Trump's wives—Ivana and Melania—worked as models, and in between he was married to Marla, an aspiring actress who later appeared on and off-Broadway. So it's no surprise to learn that Trump introduced his son Don Jr to his wife Vanessa, a model who appeared in the 2003 film *Something's Gotta Give*. (Hollywood: good except for politics.) Even better, she is a former Miss USA—the beauty pageant Trump owns—from 2004. Before Don Jr, Vanessa dated Leonard DiCaprio.

We are not going to speculate if Donald ever met Vanessa in a dressing room.

Eric Trump's wife Lara worked in television (also very good!) as a story coordinator and later producer for *Inside Edition*, a show that focuses on tabloid news. She is a university graduate who also attended the French Culinary Institute in New York. (France: not so good.)

Ivanka, of course, married Jared Kushner, himself from a family with its own empire estimated to be worth $1.8 billion, according to *Forbes*. About half of it is in real estate, with the rest coming from a health insurance company Jared founded in 2012, the *New York Observer* (now online only), which he purchased in 2006, and cash and investments worth $420 million.[1]

---

1  Sorvino, Chloe. 'Here's How Much Jared Kushner And His Family Are Really Worth.' *Forbes*, 22 Feb. 2017, https://goo.gl/Hzjw6s.

# 19. THE TRUMPS HAVE A HISTORY OF RACISM

Fred Trump might be best remembered by the average New Yorker for being sued by the US Department of Justice in 1973 for violating fair housing laws.

As owners of the Trump Organization, Fred and Donald were accused of discriminating against black people who applied to let Trump-owned flats. The test case came from a biracial couple: the husband, who was black, was turned down to rent a flat, while his wife, a white woman, was approved at the same complex and with the same credentials.

True to form, the Trumps countersued the government for $100 million for making false statements about the company. Their lawyer was Roy Cohn, a key player in the so-called Red Scare that gripped the US in the 1950s, and who prosecuted Julius and Ethel Rosenberg who were found guilty of spying for the Soviet Union and put to death. Later, as a staff attorney for the House Un-American Activities Committee, Cohn helped ruined the lives of countless citizens it accused of harboring 'Communist sympathies.'

By the 1970s, Cohn was wreaking havoc in private practice; a profile in *Esquire* said he was the lawyer of choice for 'clients who want to kill their husband, torture a business client, break the government's legs...he is not a very nice man.'[1]

Nearly two years later, the Trumps settled the case out of court with the Justice Department, which required them to 'acquaint themselves personally on a detailed basis' with US fair housing laws. They were also instructed to place advertisements in local papers to inform minority groups that they had an equal opportunity to let from Trump-owned properties. The Trumps, of course, considered it a win for them since they didn't have to admit actual guilt.

Fred is also remembered for getting caught up in radical right-wing politics as the nation headed toward the Depression. On Memorial Day (Remembrance Day elsewhere) 1927, he joined

---

1 Auletta, Ken. 'Don't Mess With Roy Cohn.' *Esquire*, 5 Dec. 1978.

an anti-Catholic Ku Klux Klan march in Queens and was one of seven men arrested for failing to follow police orders to disperse. According to reports at the time, all the men arrested were wearing Klan regalia.

During the Second World War, Fred worried that his German heritage would harm his reputation with Jewish tenants and sought to conceal it, telling people his family were Swedes. (Donald continued the fabrication in his ghostwritten autobiography *The Art of the Deal*.)

The apple didn't fall too far from the tree. In 1991, Donald Trump told staff at the Trump Plaza Hotel and Casino in Atlantic City, New Jersey, to keep black employees away from a craps table where a mobster named Robert LiButtu was playing. LiButtu was a notorious racist who would go into rages with racist expletives when he lost, and was also known for using foul language about women. After receiving complaints from nine employees, the New Jersey Casino Control Commission fined Trump Plaza $200,000 for violating state anti-discrimination laws.[2]

---

2  Mathis-Lilley, Ben. 'Hey Look, Here's Another Incredibly Sleazy Thing Donald Trump Was Involved With in the '80s.' *Slate*, 8 Mar. 2016, https://goo.gl/a6iVKh.

## 20. WOODY GUTHRIE WROTE A SONG ABOUT FRED TRUMP

Donald was not the first Trump to get noticed by popular culture. His conservative, strait-laced father Fred beat him to it.

In 1950, Woody Guthrie—the most celebrated American folk singer of his time and perhaps of all time—rewrote one of his most famous songs to criticize his landlord, who was none other than Fred Trump. Guthrie lambasted 'old man Trump' for barring black veterans from flats Fred Trump built with government funds specifically provided to develop affordable housing for World War II ex-servicemen.

Guthrie, himself a veteran, signed a lease to move into a Trump development of flats called Beach Haven (not to be confused with a New Jersey beach town) in the Brooklyn neighborhood of Coney Island in 1950. Coney Island has long been a retreat for New Yorkers seeking to escape summer heat for a day or two at the beach. It's famous for its boardwalk, Nathan's hot dogs, amusement park, and seashore. The US government selected it as an ideal location for veterans with families.

Guthrie regularly spoke out against racism in American society in his songs and participated in rallies to protest mob attacks on black Americans. He was furious to discover after moving in that his new neighborhood had no black residents because the Trumps refused to allow black tenants.

Will Kaufman, a professor of American Literature and Culture at the University of Central Lancashire, discovered this while researching the Guthrie archive at the University of Oklahoma. He wrote about it for *The Conversation*, a news site for academics, in 2016.[1]

Trump's Beach Haven development had what was called a 'restrictive covenant' that twisted the government's Federal Housing Authority guideline to avoid 'inharmonious use of housing' to justify a ban against non-white tenants.

1 Kaufman, Will. 'Woody Guthrie, 'Old Man Trump' and a Real Estate Empire's Racist Foundations.'*The Conversation*, 8 Nov. 2017, https://goo.gl/ShdMmq.

Restrictive covenants were in wide use throughout the US to bar Jews as well from moving into 'redlined' neighborhoods either as tenants or homeowners. These covenants were actually declared illegal by the US Supreme Court in 1948 but it took another 20 years for Congress to pass legislation that specifically barred covenants based on racial, ethnic, or religious prejudices on properties developed with government funds.

Guthrie's notebooks referred to his new neighborhood as 'Bitch Haven', Professor Kaufman says. He wrote verses about integrating the area, and viewed Fred Trump as the epitome of racial hatred. 'Old Man Trump...drawed that color line here at his eighteen hundred family project,' he fumed.[1]

Guthrie was so angry, Kaufman learned, that he actually rewrote lyrics to one of his most famous songs, *I Ain't Got No Home*, to target his landlord:

> 'Beach Haven ain't my home!
> I just cain't [sic] pay the rent!
> My money's down the drain!
> And my soul is badly bent!
> Beach Haven looks like heaven
> Where no black ones come to roam!
> No, no, no! Old Man Trump!
> Old Beach Haven ain't my home!

You can see the full lyrics at http://woodyguthrie.org/Lyrics/Old_Man_Trump.htm

A singer named Ryan Harvey recorded a video of Guthrie's song that you can see on You Tube at https://www.youtube.com/watch?v=TmZnlGBhwKg.

# 21. A 'MR BARRON' EXISTED LONG BEFORE TRUMP'S YOUNGEST CHILD

Donald Trump has a history with the name Barron that stretches back long before his youngest child was born.

Trump's first 'Barron' was Barron Hilton, who sold him the Atlantic City Hilton Hotel in 1985 for about $300 million, information disclosed to *The New York Times* by 'John Baron', identified as a spokesperson for the Trump Organization.[1]

From the 1970s through the 1990s, reporters in New York spoke on the phone with Trump spokesmen or executives named 'John Barron' (sometimes spelled with one 'r') or 'John Miller.' Funny thing was, neither showed up at any of the Trump events, and between the casinos, hotels, beauty pageants, etc., there were a lot of events one would expect to see at least one of these blokes.

That's because, as more than a few reporters suspected, they were actually Donald Trump, *The Washington Post* reported in May, 2016. Reporters who spoke with the *Post* remember 'unusually helpful and boastful advocates' of Trump.

Trump apparently began using the name 'Mr. Barron' when he first joined his father's business and hearing him speak as 'Mr. Green' to reporters. He finally owned up to Barron's true identity after a witness testified during a 1990 lawsuit that a 'Mr. Barron' had threatened to sue him if he didn't drop clients he was representing in a lawsuit against Trump for underpaying them.

'The Barron' was also a code name Trump used when he left messages for Marla Maples while he was still married to and living with Ivana.[2]

*The Times* identified 'John Baron' as a vice president of The Trump Organization in a 1985 article about Trump asking other owners of the now-defunct United States Football League to help

---

1  Saxon, Wolfgang. 'Trump Buys Hilton's Hotel In Atlantic City.' *The New York Times*, 27 Apr. 1985, www.nytimes.com/1985/04/28/nyregion/trump-buys-hilton-s-hotel-in-atlantic-city.html.

2  Fisher, Marc, and Will Hobson. 'Donald Trump Masqueraded as Publicist to Brag about Himself.' *The Washington Post*, 13 May 2016, https://goo.gl/euhVWU.

him pay the $8.25 million salary for his team's quarterback. (Fact #66 has more information about this venture.)

Earlier, 'John Baron' had defended Trump to *The Times* over his decision to destroy Art Deco sculptures on the Bonwit Teller Building he was demolishing to make way for Trump Tower.[2]

A real Barron joined the Trump clan on March 20, 2006. As the world knows, he and his mother delayed moving to the White House until the 2016–17 school year ended in New York. He attends a private day school in Maryland, plays golf with his father, and speaks Slovene, his mother's first language.

## 22. TRUMP CHILDREN ARE NOT ALLOWED TO HAVE PETS

Trumps do not have pets. Donald and his siblings didn't have pets growing up. He hasn't had a pet as an adult and barely tolerated Ivana's poodle Chappy. For the first time in over 100 years, there are no pets in the White House or plans to get one.

Barack Obama entered the White House petless, but had famously promised his daughters the night he was elected that they would get the puppy he promised them. Bo arrived within the year, and later, they adopted Sunny as well. George W Bush's dog Barney shot videos as he scampered around the White House. Bill Clinton's family had their beloved cat Socks, later joined by Buddy the Dog. George H W Bush had Millie, an English springer spaniel once named the Ugliest Dog in Washington by the *Washingtonian* magazine, who co-authored books with Barbara Bush.

A Trump friend, Lois Pope, picked out what she thought would be a perfect dog for the Trump family. Patton—named for the World War II General George Patton, who Trump says is his favorite general—is a Goldendoodle who's loyal, beautiful (both very, very important things to be in Trumpworld), and to top it off, hypoallergenic. Pope introduced Patton to Trump and his son Barron at Mar-a-Lago, where she is a longtime member. Trump told her he was too busy to have a dog.

This might have been good for Patton, because Trump doesn't show any appreciation for dogs. In fact, he uses their name in vain when he's up for tweeting insults, as the *Huffington Post* pointed out:

'@BrentBozell [a conservative activist]…came to me begging for money like a dog.'
[Fox News television presenter] 'Glenn Beck got fired like a dog' – 12/16/15
'Robert Pattinson should not take back Kristen Stewart. She cheated on him like a dog.' – 10/17/12[1]

1 Graber, Anna. 'Why Doesn't Donald Trump Own a Dog?' *Huffington Post*, 17 April 2017, http://www.huffingtonpost.ca/amyrose-lane/where-is-the-first-dog_b_16017530.html.

More recently, Trump tweeted that Senator Bob Corker, a Republican from Tennessee, couldn't get elected 'dog catcher.' Corker has challenged Trump on several issues and has decided not to run for re-election.

Wealthy people often own horses; why not Trump, or at least Melania and Barron? Perhaps Trump would enjoy falconry; that's at least as macho as Vladimir Putin strutting around bare-chested and leading a tiger on a leash. Though the attack by the bald eagle called Uncle Sam on the presidential candidate during an ill-advised photo op in December 2015 suggests otherwise. The symbol of America, bald (but actually not), ruffling the lacquered feathers of a frankly terrified Donald; there's just too much going on here, synecdochically speaking.

Medical sociologist Joan Liebermann-Smith wrote about petless people back in 2011. Her findings indicate that by not having a pet, Trump may be subconsciously distancing himself from his peers. Pet owners, she wrote, are more likely to be white, married, have children, be employed full-time, own a home, and have a higher income.

Liebermann-Smith cited studies that found children who grow up with pets are more likely to be empathic, nurturing, and have better social skills. A dog or two in the Trump household in Queens would have been a good idea.[2]

Maybe Barron caught his own pet, like the Bill the Lizard who belonged to Teddy Roosevelt's children. Bill eventually made his home in the honeysuckles that grew around the front of the White House.

2 Liebermann-Smith, Joan. 'Petless People: A Breed Apart?' *Huffington Post*, 15 June 2011, https://www.huffingtonpost.com/joan-liebmannsmith-phd/ petless-people-a-breed-ap_b_873617.html.

# 23. TRUMP USED TO BE PRETTY ARTICULATE

One of the things many Americans who were familiar with Trump even before *The Apprentice* have noticed is that his speaking abilities have noticeably deteriorated since he entered politics.

When I watched *The Apprentice*, I was struck by the comparative silence from the mogul I remembered as a glib, even articulate, attention-grabbing man about town I saw on local New York television growing up in nearby New Jersey. Like many New Yorkers, he could talk 'a mile a minute'. Listening to a few recordings released by *The Howard Stern Show*, which Trump hasn't appeared on since 2004, I'm reminded of this almost nonstop talker who barely took a breath and who could list 'fact' after 'fact' about everything from real estate to women to his plans to run for public office.

So what happened?

It could be Trump has suffered a minor, or series of minor, strokes that may not have even been recognized as such. Even small strokes have a long-term impact on speech, leading to aphasia, a condition in which a person has trouble expressing himself. Trump's uneven speech and inability (or is it disinterest?) in forming a cohesive sentence sometimes make me wonder if he has aphasia.

The news service STAT looked into this very question in May 2017 and spoke with experts in cognitive assessment and neurolinguistics, and psychologists and psychiatrists. They all agreed Trump's speech has deteriorated and some said this could reflect on Trump's brain health.

These experts noticed Trump's use of what are called 'SAT words' in the US ('A-levels' would be a rough equivalent) in the last century. He used to use words like 'inclination', 'discredited', 'contentious', and 'adversity'. Today, he uses simpler word like 'loser', 'liar', and 'sad!' He repeats himself, and says 'OK' every fourth or fifth word while he tries to assemble a clear statement or more often, rebuttal.

The experts STAT interviewed say this is common during the aging process. Linguistic and cognitive declines often happen together because both work from the brain's prefrontal cortex, which processes higher cognitive functions like memory, judgment, and planning. Without testing Trump, it's harder to make a definitive call, but he is aged 71, he is overweight, and he doesn't appear to engage in any kind of vigorous exercise (he uses a golf cart when he's on the course). Reading is said to keep the brain engaged, but Trump has never been much of a reader. He struggled to answer then-Fox reporter Megyn Kelly's question about his favourite book, finally coming up with *All Quiet on the Western Front*.[1]

In a rambling interview with *The Hollywood Reporter* in 2016, Trump could name the topic of books he was supposedly reading, but not the books themselves. 'I'm reading the Ed Klein book on Hillary Clinton and I'm reading the book on Richard Nixon that was, well, I can get you the exact information on it.' And, he said, he was re-reading *All Quiet on the Western Front*.[2]

'It is very queer that the unhappiness of the world is so often brought on by small men.' (Erich Maria Remarque, *All Quiet on the Western Front*.)

DONALD TRUMP IN 100 FACTS

1  Begley, Sharon. 'Trump Used to Be More Articulate. What Could Explain the Change?' *STAT*, 25 July 2017, www.statnews.com/2017/05/23/donald-trump-speaking-style-interviews/.
2  Wolff, Michael. 'The Donald Trump Conversation: Politics' 'Dark Heart' Is Having the Best Time Anyone's Ever Had.' *The Hollywood Reporter*, 1 June 2016, www.hollywoodreporter.com/features/donald-trump-conversation-politics-dark-898465.

47

# 24. DON'T MUSS WITH ME: TRUMP, LIKE ALL POLITICIANS, IS HAIR TODAY, GONE TOMORROW

Long before he became President, Trump's hair was a source of much amusement. When he was younger, his hair had the popular blow-dried look of the 1970s. In fact, he was kind of cute in a baby-faced way. In the late 1980s, though, his hair changed. First, he grew it longer than you would see at the time on a conservative businessman. At one point in 1989, it curled down past his collar.

He also had a scalp reduction procedure that year, according to a deposition his first wife Ivana gave during their divorce proceedings. The procedure was unexpectedly painful and, Ivana alleged at the time, he assaulted her because she had recommended the plastic surgeon. The deposition, which had been sealed, was leaked to a writer named Harry Hurt who used it in an unauthorized 1993 biography of Trump.

How angry was Trump? Ivana stated he ripped out a chunk of her hair and worse followed. Hurt's book says he confirmed this with two of Ivana's friends.[1] Ivana later retracted the claim.

By 1992, Trump's thick locks were thinning out a bit—no big deal to a normal person, even a normal billionaire. And around this time, the hair color changed. It's one thing to cover up emerging greys but Trump, it appears, opted for an almost-punky blond.

It doesn't seem that Trump ever wore a toupee or had hair plugs. What he did do, according to Amy Lasch the stylist who tried to tame it for *The Apprentice*, was grow it really long so that he could comb it back to give the appearance of a thick mane. In an interview with *The Mirror*, Lasch said his dyed blond hair was a 'calamity.' It had not been professionally styled, unless he managed to find the world's worst stylist: 'It was not a hairdresser cutting...it was scary. It was cut in a straight line.' Lasch thinks an employee or someone in his family was responsible.

1 Hurt, Harry III. *Lost Tycoon: The Many Lives of Donald J. Trump*. Echo Point, 1993.

Trump also used a lot of hairspray, Lasch said, and would try to fix his hair himself. She would only comb the back and sides. 'But everything was solid. I tapped it with my comb and it would bounce back.'[2]

In February 2017, Harold Bornstein, Trump's long-time doctor, told *The New York Times* that Trump took finastride, a prostate-related medication also used to treat male pattern baldness. (It is marketed as Propecia for this purpose.) This would explain an earlier letter on Trump's health in which he noted a very low PSA marker for prostate cancer and that, if elected, Trump would be 'the healthiest individual ever elected to the Presidency.'

As for hair, Bornstein said 'He has all his hair. I have all my hair.'[3]

To be fair, Trump has publicly allowed people to muss up his hair, including talk show host Jimmy Fallon and various women he pulled from rally crowds to testify to its genuineness.

2 Samson, Pete. 'The truth about Donald Trump's Hair: Former hairdresser reveals the lacquer, home cuts...and if it's real.' *The Mirror*, 10 Nov. 2016.

3 Altman, M.D, and Lawrence K. 'Donald Trump's Longtime Doctor Says President Takes Hair-Growth Drug.' *The New York Times*, 1 Feb. 2017, www.nytimes.com/2017/02/01/us/politics/trump-prostate-drug-hair-harold-bornstein.html?_r=0.

## 25. TRUMP IS OVERWEIGHT

Trump is known to humiliate people he considers overweight and imagines that computer crimes are committed by fat people. But he is overweight himself.

According to a letter released by Dr Harold Bornstein, his long-time and possibly former physician, Trump weighed 236 pounds in September 2016. At six feet three inches,[1] this puts his body mass index (BMI) endorsed by the National Heart, Lung, and Blood Institute at 29.5. This is considered overweight and just under the marker for obesity, which is set at 30 or greater.

Trump certainly doesn't eat like someone who cares about weight or nutrition. *The Washington Post* reports he's a regular at McDonald's—where he eats hamburgers, not salads—and is known to enjoy Kentucky Fried Chicken on his private jet. (The *Post* is among the media that have been occasionally banned from the White House Press Room and from Air Force One as well as the campaign jet.)[2]

Many casual observers noticed that Trump wore ugly anoraks during his trips to hurricane-devastated areas, which he probably thinks hide his weight. (Even Obama looked ridiculous in the anoraks with the Presidential seal.) He could have worn a nice Burberry's trench coat.

Photos of his weekend golf outings show a hefty older guy wearing tight clothing. In June 2017, social media had a little fun with close-up photos of Trump's wristwatch, which looked tight enough for a blood draw. There was even a Twitter account @TrumpsWatchBand that tweeted 'Sometimes I pretend I'm an Apple Watch and Beyoncé is wearing me. And then morning comes and those little hands take me again.'

1 'Bornstein Letters of Health for Trump.' *The New York Times*, 1 Feb. 2017, www.nytimes.com/interactive/2017/02/01/us/politics/document-Bornstein-Letter-of-Health-for-Trump.html.

2 Sietsema, Tom. 'The world is Trump's Oyster but he prefers Filet-O-Fish.' *The Washington Post*, 24 Mar. 2016, https://www.washingtonpost.com/lifestyle/food/trump-can-afford-to-eat-the-finest-food-instead-he-eats-the-most-generic/2016/03/24/

# 26. TRUMP IS MR MYSOPHOBIA

Everyone is afraid of something. Donald Trump is afraid of germs.

This is kind of understandable when you live in a dense city like New York or Washington where the flu will spread in hours and empty offices for days. (Fewer people there question the value of flu vaccines.) Trump's germ phobia extends to pressing elevator buttons—and remember, his private home is atop the 72-story Trump Tower where the elevators have 90 buttons. Not to mention he's a politician, which normally demands handshakes and kissing babies.

Germ phobia might also explain his crude and immature comments about women's bodily fluids.

Trump's germ phobia became news just before his inauguration when a widespread and unverified rumor came out that he watched Russian prostitutes engage in everyday common bodily functions in the Presidential suite at the Moscow Ritz-Carlton, the same suite where President and Mrs Obama once stayed during an official visit. This was part of the Steele Dossier provided by ex-British spy Christopher Steele that was initially funded by a Washington, DC 'operations research' firm, later by a conservative newspaper, and later still allegedly by the Clinton campaign. Its contents became widely known to Washington power brokers on both sides of the aisle, including President Obama and senior Senate Republicans.

Trump angrily denied the story at a press conference, adding that he's a 'very much a germaphobe, by the way. Believe me.' Still, he was upset enough about the supposed video to have reportedly discussed it with his temporary National Security Advisor Michael Flynn[1]

He also told the press conference that he knows enough to be on his best behavior while overseas: 'In those room, you have cameras in the strangest places, cameras that are so small with modern technology, you can't see them and won't know...I was in Russia

---

1 Miere, Jason Le. 'Trump and Comey Talked Russian 'Hookers' and 'Golden Shower' Allegations.' *Newsweek*, 7 June 2017, www.newsweek.com/ trump-comey-hookers-golden-showers-622604.

years ago with the Miss Universe Contest, which did very well, Moscow, the Moscow area, did very well.'

So how does the President of the United States deal with his germ phobia? He avoids shaking hands as much as possible, limiting it to greeting foreign dignitaries. Aides often carry hand sanitizer for him.

In his 1997 book *The Art of the Comeback*, Trump called handshaking 'one of the curses of American society...I happen to be a clean hands freak. I feel much better after I thoroughly wash my hands, which I do as much as possible.'[2]

Does Trump also have obsessive-compulsive disorder? Frequent hand washing is a trademark for this fairly common condition. He has also been known to get in a daylong bad mood over a limo driver's mismatched shoes and suit or have a tantrum over a staffer's scuffed shoes.[3]

Trump's germ phobia is also reported to be the reason he favors mass-produced and processed fast food because such food outlets have more to lose from a story about a bad hamburger, for example. (He's right: in 2016, the Chipotle chain closed all its 1900-plus locations after an outbreak of E. coli and has never recovered.) Trump's preference for steaks cooked well done is another example of his efforts to avoid contamination.

2  Trump, Donald. *The Art of the Comeback*, Times Books, 1997.

## 27. TRUMP INSISTED HE OWNS A RENOIR; HE MIGHT STILL THINK IT'S GENUINE

Tim O'Brien is a journalist who has written extensively on Trump. In 2005, he published a biography somewhat presciently titled *Trump Nation: The Art of Being the Donald*.

One item O'Brien didn't mention in the book is that Trump believes he owns a painting by French Impressionist Pierre-Auguste Renoir. O'Brien remembered enough of the conversation to relay it to *Vanity Fair* in 2016. He says he asked Trump, who had it hanging in his private plane at the time, if it was the original. 'Yes,' Trump answered. 'Donald, it's not,' O'Brien says he told him. 'I grew up in Chicago, that Renoir is called "Two Sisters on the Terrace" and it's hanging on a wall at the Art Institute of Chicago. That's not an original.'[1]

The *Vanity Fair* interview caught the attention of the Art Institute, which told the *Chicago Tribune* that they're certain theirs is the real thing. It was gifted to them in 1933 by the estate of Anne Swann Coburn, an art collector who purchased the painting from a dealer who bought it from Renoir himself. After her husband Lewis, a patent attorney, died in 1910, Coburn moved into a swanky Chicago hotel where she displayed most of her art. (She used a Degas as a fireplace screen and kept one of Van Gogh's Arles paintings under her bed.) In all, her estate donated over 70 late 19th- and early 20th-century paintings to the Chicago Art Institute.

Which means Trump bought a fake Renoir, probably at great expense. He's told people that it's worth $10 million. You can see it in photographs taken in the Trump suite.

Two art historians were willing to go on the record about Trump's painting for *ArtNet News*. They separately studied a photo of Melania Trump posing in front of the painting and are convinced it's a copy. Both also stated that Renoir never made copies of his own work.[2]

---

1 Bilton, Nick. 'Donald Trump's Fake Renoir: The Untold Story.' *Vanity Fair*, 16 Oct. 2017, www.vanityfair.com/news/2017/10/donald-trumps-fake-renoir.

Trump has also once claimed another Renoir, 'La Loge', which is actually in the Courtauld Art Institute in London.[2]

Speaking of fakes, Trump says that he invented the actual word! In October 2017, he sat down with Mike Huckabee for an interview with the Christian network TBN. During the interview, Trump sort of claimed that he invented, or at least popularized, the word 'fake' in his description of the mainstream media in the US. 'I guess other people have used it over the years, but I've never noticed it.'[3]

'Fake,' according to *Salon's* research with Mirriam-Webster, dates to the 15th century and has been documented in the American vernacular since the late 1800s.[4]

Huckabee is the former governor of Arkansas who twice tried ran for the Republican nomination for President. He is also the father of the current White House Press Secretary Sarah Huckabee Sanders, whose escapades are chronicled in Fact #91.

2 Boucher, Brian. 'Donald Trump Bragged About the Renoir on His Private Jet. Experts Say It's a Fake. *Artnet News*, News, 20 Oct. 2017, news.artnet.com/art-world/donald-trump-fake-renoir-1117814.

3 'Gov. Mike Huckabee's Full Interview with President Trump,' uploaded by TBN. 7 October 2017, https://youtu.be/hVQPVGPAUtc.

4 Holloway, Kali. '5 Things Trump Said He Invented, but Didn't.' *Salon*, 13 Oct. 2017, www.salon.com/2017/10/13/5-things-trump-said-he-invented-but-didnt_partner/.

# 28. TRUMP HAD A CRUSH ON PRINCESS DIANA

Television journalist and presenter Selina Scott can tell you a few things about Trump. She first met him in 1995 to interview him for an ITV profile. As she told biographer Michael D'Antonio, she rather liked him at first but eventually concluded that Trump was someone who 'got his own way by treating people appallingly.'

The documentary ended up being quite critical of Trump, who characteristically reacted by lashing out, sending notes to Scott that he made public to tell her she was 'boring,' 'obnoxious,' 'very sleazy' and 'unattractive.' (The word 'projecting' springs to mind.) There were references to her 'fading image' and 'little talent...even fewer viewers.' Worst of all, she was no longer 'hot,' the ultimate Trump insult.[1]

The documentary aired just once. It will be interesting to see if it ever resurfaces.

Around this time, Scott's friend Princess Diana phoned her to ask what she should do about Donald Trump sending her flowers. Her Kensington Palace residence was overflowing with them, at a time when she was separated from Prince Charles but not yet divorced. Scott says the Princess was more than a little concerned that Trump was stalking her. 'I told her to just bin the lot.'[1]

Diana had met Trump a few times at charity functions and shared a table with him and his second wife, Marla Maples, when United Cerebral Palsy named her Humanitarian of the Year in 1995. At the time, she was dating another member of the billionaire club, Theodore Forstmann.

After her divorce from Prince Charles, Trump starting sending her even larger bouquets and, Scott says, Diana told her Trump was giving her 'the creeps'. Trump, Scott believes, saw Diana as the ultimate trophy wife.[2]

Just weeks after Diana's death in 1997, Trump managed to degrade the late Princess by discussing her with American

---

1 D'Antonio, *Never Enough*, 2015.
2 Glancy, Josh. 'Mogul 'Sought Trophy Wife'.' *The Times & The Sunday Times*, The Sunday Times, 16 Aug. 2015, www.thetimes.co.uk/article/mogul-sought-trophy-wife-lbdfn7rxngr.

shock-jock Howard Stern, on whose radio show he's made frequent appearances. Tapes released in 2016 unfold a conversation in which Stern goads Trump into bragging that he could have 'gotten Lady Di' (I'm putting a polite spin on Stern's actual words). He went on to talk about how attractive Diana was: 'A thought she was supermodel beautiful.' He also claimed he did a 'personal favor' for Diana and that she wrote him a 'really nice letter...the most beautiful warm letter' thanking him for it a couple of months before she died. (He also said he sent her 'some flowers.')[3]

Stern still maintains that he and Trump are friends although Trump's last appearance on the show was in 2004.

In 2007, Trump decided enough time had passed to treat the late Princess as just a lost opportunity for conquest. In a discussion of his 'top ten' most beautiful women, Trump said he would have slept with Diana 'without hesitation,' adding 'she was crazy, but those are minor details.' 'I only have one regret,' Trump told Stern, 'that I never had the opportunity to court Lady Diana Spencer.'[4]

3 The Howard Stern Show. *Interview with Donald Trump*. 1997. https://soundcloud.com/buzzfeedandrew/trump-on-princess-diana
4 The Howard Stern Show. *Interview with Donald Trump*. 2000. https://soundcloud.com/buzzfeedandrew/trumps-top-10-women

## 29. TRUMP REALLY IS SENSITIVE ABOUT HIS FINGERS: BLAME *SPY*

*Spy* was a New York-based satirical magazine that ran off and on between 1987 and 1998. It targeted lots of celebrities but Donald Trump always held a special place in the *Spy* heart. The feeling might be mutual, since Trump tweeted a series of attacks on *Spy* after the tragic murders of *Charlie Hebdo* staff in January 2015 and 17 years after the magazine folded.

*Spy* first targeted Trump and his fingers in 1988 introducing him to readers as 'a short-fingered vulgarian,' former contributing editor Bruce Feirstein reminisced in a 2015 article for *Vanity Fair*. *Spy*'s editors Graydon Carter and Kurt Andersen targeted him because they 'recognized Trump for what he was: a bombastic, self-aggrandizing, un-self aware bully.'[1]

Trump made the first of many threats to sue the magazine. He also sent over a copy of *The Art of the Deal*, with his hand outlined on the cover to indicate he wasn't short-fingered, and a note: 'If you hit me, I will hit you back 100 times harder.'[1]

The following year, *Spy* put Trump on the cover for its November issue, with the headline 'WA-A-A-A-H! Little Donald — Unhappy at Last.' It featured a pre-Photoshop image of Trump's face atop a child waving its arms in a tantrum. The caption read *Trump's Final Days, Page 50* for the cover story, a fact-check of *The Art of the Deal*.

Trump made another appearance on the *Spy* cover in August 1990. Here, Trump is shown perched on a box listing inside articles including *Donald Trump, A Heck of a Guy* and, ironically, *It's Fun to Live in Queens*.

Ivana was actually on *Spy*'s cover before Donald. An extreme close-up photo of her was featured on the May 1989 cover, headlined *An Investigative Tribute: Ivanarama!*

Someone on Marco Rubio's staff must have discovered the nearly-30-year old joke during the days when it seemed like

---

1 Feirstein, Bruce. 'Trump's War On.' *The Hive*, Vanity Fair, 12 Aug. 2015, www.vanityfair.com/news/2015/08/spy-vs-trump.

there were at least 17 Republicans vying for the nomination. Rubio, smarting after Trump called him 'Little Marco' at a rally, responded with his own taunt: 'You know what they say about guys with small hands.' The Salem, Virginia crowd, which NBC reported responded with 'stunned laughter,' finally clapped after Rubio answered his own riddle; 'You can't trust 'em!'[2]

Trump decided to deflect the finger of suspicion during a televised debate a week later. 'He hit my hands,' Trump said, holding them up for inspection. 'Nobody has ever hit my hands. I have never heard of this. Are they small hands'? Before anyone could answer, Trump spun to face Rubio. 'If they are small, something else must be small. I guarantee you there is no problem. I guarantee.'[3]

Of course Trump had heard of the small hands taunt. He'd never forgotten *Spy* or Graydon Carter, who says Trump continued to send occasional 'fan mail. Trump sends him photos of himself, with his hands circled in gold Sharpie pen. 'I almost feel sorry for the poor fellow because to me, the fingers still look abnormally stubby.'[3]

2  Alexandra Jaffe. 'Donald Trump Has 'Small Hands,' Marco Rubio Says.' *NBCNews.com*, 29 Feb. 2016, www.nbcnews.com/politics/2016-election/donald-trump-has-small-hands-marco-rubio-says-n527791.

3  Carter, Blame Graydon. 'The Joke about Donald Trump's Hands Goes Back Nearly 30 Years.' *CNNMoney*, 4 Mar. 2016, money.cnn.com/2016/03/04/media/donald-trump-fingers-hands/index.html.

# 30. ROY COHN, ONE OF THE MOST INFAMOUS AMERICANS IN MODERN HISTORY, WAS TRUMP'S OTHER MENTOR

Fred Trump Sr was Donald's primary mentor growing up and in his early days in business. His other mentor was Roy Cohn, who many Americans remember as a key part of the 1950s Red Scare that ruined the lives of countless citizens, as previously mentioned.

Roy Cohn started his legal career as an Assistant US Attorney in Manhattan, specializing in prosecuting accused Soviet spies and Communist party members. He came to national attention in 1951 at the trial of Julius and Ethel Rosenberg, who were accused of giving the Soviet Union stolen classified documents about the nuclear bomb. Cohn questioned Ethel's brother, whose testimony was central to their conviction. The Rosenbergs were executed in 1953.

The brother later said he lied on the stand but most historians agree the couple was guilty. The trial was littered with judicial and legal misconduct, most of it from Cohn. Cohn later bragged that the death penalty was due to his influence with the sentencing judge.

Soon after the trial, the notorious FBI director J Edgar Hoover, a relentless Communist hunter, recommended Cohn to assist Senator Joseph McCarthy, who was investigating everyone from low-level government clerks to Hollywood screenwriters to Army generals for Communist sympathies. The two launched the disastrous Army-McCarthy hearings of 1954 that were broadcast on live TV. This was the first time many Americans could actually see Congress in action, and many were aghast. The media coverage contributed to McCarthy's downfall and Cohn slunk away to make his fortune in New York. There, he represented a variety of clients that included Mafia leaders, the Catholic Church, wealthy club owners caught dealing drugs, and the New York Yankees baseball team. He also represented the Duke and Duchess of Windsor and Aristotle Onassis.

Trump met Roy Cohn in 1973 at Le Club, a private discotheque that attracted aging wealthy men and beautiful young people seeking mutually beneficial relationships. He and Fred hired Cohn to defend them against a government lawsuit for discriminating against black applicants to let their flats (see Fact #19 for details). When Cohn's counter-suit for $100 million was dismissed, he wrote the judge a letter calling her a 'hot-tempered white female!' Later, he accused her of 'Gestapo-like tactics' (both he and the judge were Jewish).

Trump, of course, loved the drama. Biographers Kranish and Fischer say the two became inseparable. Cohn advised Trump on how to deal with the media and helped him get mentioned in the Murdoch-owned *New York Post's* Page Six gossip column. He negotiated on Trump's behalf with New York's power elite and put together his prenuptial agreement for Ivana.

In 1984, Cohn announced he had liver cancer but actually had AIDS. Trump and many others were long aware Cohn was gay, but pulled away from him at the time. 'Donald pisses ice water,' Cohn fumed.

In 1986, Cohn was disbarred for unethical behavior, thus losing his right to appear in court. He died five weeks later.

1 Kranish and Fischer, *Trump Revealed*, 2016.

# 31. TRUMP USED TO BE VERY FOND OF THE MEDIA!

The President who attacks the media at every opportunity used to be very fond of what political scientists call The Fourth Estate.

In his book *The Art of the Deal*, Trump discussed the value of feeding news tidbits to media, writing that positive aspects of being in the news far outweigh any drawbacks.

Working with the notorious attorney Roy Cohn, Trump honed his media skills. Tabloid papers like the *New York Daily News* and the *New York Post* regularly featured him and whatever wife or girlfriend he was with. Business publications like *Forbes* and *The Wall Street Journal* (now owned by Rupert Murdoch) profiled his projects.

As Michael Kranish and Marc Fisher write, he developed a knack for 'laundering quotes or rumors.' He could persuade reporters to simply attribute something he didn't want personally connected to him from 'a source within the Trump Organization' and created a couple of aliases, John Barron and John Miller.[1] (Trump's middle name is John.)

Nothing, though, could have prepared anyone for the media circus that surrounded Trump's first divorce. The *Post* outdid itself with a February 1990 headline of a remark attributed to Marla Maples: 'BEST SEX I'VE EVER HAD!' The next day, the rival *Daily News* reported Donald was been 'delighted' by the headline.[1]

Sometimes Trump's media manipulation backfired. In 1991, *People*'s Trump/Ivana/Marla reporter received back-to-back calls from men who identified themselves as John Barron and John Miller. Barron's news: Trump had dumped Marla Maples. Then Miller called to dish about Trump's next love interest and named several women, including Madonna. The reporter thought they both sounded like Trump and called Maples to play her the recordings. Maples confirmed Trump's voice on both and burst into tears.[1]

---

1 Kranish and Fisher, *Trump Revealed*, 2016.

As Trump's behavior grew more outlandish and he indulged in 'birther' and other rumors, the media began milking his entertainment value. Did they inadvertently create a working-class hero out of Trump? The debate remains hotly argued.

One thing's for sure: once he faced media criticism or tough questioning, Trump hit back. Since taking office, he has occasionally banished television cameras from the White House Press Room and even barred reporters from *The New York Times*, *The Los Angeles Times*, CNN, and Politico from off-camera briefings. At the same time, he admitted *Breitbart News*, the 'home for the alt-right' according to his former advisor Stephen Bannon, who ran the site before his tenure with Trump and has since returned.

Trump has repeatedly called *The New York Times* a 'failing' newspaper. In fact, the *Times* had its best-ever quarter for new subscriptions in 2017, attracting 308,000 digital subscribers in the first quarter.[2] Its stock value rose 30%.[3]

After Trump became President, *The Washington Post* added this header to its front page: 'Democracy Dies in Darkness.'

2 Stelter, Brian. 'New York Times Has Record Subscriber Growth—and Some Bad News Too.' CNN Money, 3 May. 2017, money.cnn.com/2017/05/03/media/new-york-times-subscriber-growth/index.html.

3 LaMonica, Paul L. 'Trump Says NYT 'Failing'—but Stock up 30% since Election.' CNN Money, 29 Mar. 2017, money.cnn.com/2017/03/29/media/donald-trump-new-york-times-stock/?iid=EL.

## 32. TRUMP INSPIRES SOME PRETTY CLEVER COMMENTS FROM COMEDIANS AND JOURNALISTS

It's hard to qualify the funniest comments made about Trump. My personal favorites come from Alec Baldwin's amazing impression of Trump on Saturday Night Live, which you can review for yourself here: http://www.nbc.com/saturday-night-live/cast/alec-baldwin-57921/impersonation/donald-trump-285097. (The sketches are written by Brian Tucker and Tim Herlihy and no doubt helped Baldwin win his fourth Emmy in 2017.)

Here are a few utterances from Alec as Donald:

'The thing about the blacks is that they're killing each other. All the blacks live on one street in Chicago. All on one street. I just read it this morning. It's called Hell Street and they're on Hell Street, and they're all just killing each other.'

'Every day I turn on the news, and all of the newscasters are making me look so bad...by taking all of the things I say and all of the things I do and putting them on TV.'

'I do not want to talk about the pee-pee. I want to talk about what is really important, which is jobs...I am going to bring back a thick stream of jobs to this country, the biggest, strongest, steadiest stream you've ever seen. This country will be literally showered with jobs. I am a major whizz at jobs.'

Comedian Conan O'Brien:
'Nearly 70% of Americans said a Trump presidency would make them anxious. And 30% said it would make them Canadian.'

'This weekend, Donald Trump tried to win over black voters by asking them, "What the hell do you have to lose?" Coincidentally, that's also the way he proposed to all three of his wives.'

*New Yorker* humorist Andy Borowitz:
'Any time a candidate has to devote time to itemizing the differences between him and Hitler...should be kind of a red flag to voters.'

*New York Times* columnist Maureen Dowd:
'For centuries, women were considered temperamentally and biologically unsuited to hold higher office, or even to vote. So now in this campaign, we have a candidate who gets their feelings hurt very easily, is pouty and gossipy and bitchy, sometimes hysterical, worries constantly about hair care—*and it's not the woman.*'

*Last Week Tonight* host John Oliver:
'Incredibly, we may be on the brink of electing such a damaged, sociopathic narcissist that the simple presidential duty of comforting the families of fallen soldiers may actually be beyond his capabilities.'

Journalist Ronan Farrow:
'"Those who are preaching hate in our country will be asked to leave," says Donald Trump, not understanding the concept of irony.'

@OhNoSheTwitnt
'Trump is blaming Sanders supporters for the violence at his rally because you can't truly be a Hitler unless you blame a Jew for your problems.'

@behindyourback (Maura Quint)
'Someone drew a swastika on Trump's star on the Walk of Fame & there's no way to know if it was done by someone who hates him or supports him.'

Let's give Hillary the last word, a simple observation, taken from one of the debates (remember, she won the popular vote by more than 3 million):
'I know you live in your own reality, but those are not the facts.'

# 33. TRUMP HAS CHANGED AMERICAN ENGLISH LIKE NO ONE BEFORE

Trump's communication skills are undeniable even if his choice of words outrages, confuses, and mystifies—sometimes all at once.

It's difficult to catalog the most obnoxious statements Trump has made, since he seems to outdo himself nearly every week. And it's hard to be objective. One person's reaction to offensive talk about women is another's shrug toward 'locker room talk.' Who knew golf club locker rooms were such dens of vice?

One thing we can all agree on is that Trump has brought uncouth speech into public forums. But it's so hard to decide on the most offensive language he's brought into the spotlight. Luckily, Redha Medjellekh, a choreographer and TV host from France, created a video in which a more objective view of Trump's most awful statements to date is displayed through dance.

Redha released *Dancers vs Trump Quotes* in June 2017 when he was an artist-in-residence at 836M, an art gallery in San Francisco. He worked with local dancers—ballet, hip-hop—whose physical appearances match Trump quotes that people he surveyed told him they found most offensive. So a black ballerina gracefully leaps halfway across a street under a Trump quote that 'laziness is a trait in blacks,' while a white female hip-hop dancer is halted by what might be perhaps the most infamous Trump quote of all regarding how to grab women. A graceful male dancer who appears to be Latino spins and kneels under the 'Mexican rapist' quote...you get the picture. The video makes quite an impression. It's on Redha's Facebook page at https://www.facebook.com/redisdancing/videos/1911676159044435/.

Linguists have noticed Trump avoids big words most other politicians use. He's simplified (or if you will, dumbed down) American speech into sound bites and 140 characters, now expanded to 280. The progressive news website *Think Progress* spoke to word experts (i.e., linguists) who found that of Trump's thirteen most-used words, his favorite by a country mile is 'I.' 'Trump' is his fourth-favorite, reflecting his tendency to speak in both first and third person.

Eight of those 13 favorite words are single syllables
Two are double-syllables: 'money,' 'China'
One is a triple-syllable: 'Mexico'[1]

Those who follow Trump through his Twitter feed are occasionally treated to new words, such as 'covfefe,' introduced at 12:16 am US Eastern Time on May 31, 2017. 'Despite the negative press covfefe.'

The nation was thrown into a tizzy trying to uncover what this means. Looking at Trump's previous Tweet about his son-in-law Jared Kushner *not* meeting with Russians, it's a good bet that he either mistyped the word 'coverage' or more likely, Siri didn't understand his diction. (Alert Twitter followers noticed in March 2017 that Trump replaced his unsecured Samsung mobile with an iPhone—even though he called for a boycott of Apple products in 2015.)

Trump's other major linguistic contribution is the word 'bigly,' first used during the final Presidential debate to describe his immigration plan. He may have said 'big league,' a New Yorker-ish phrase. But it turns out that 'bigly' is a word although Dictonary. com says it's archaic.

1 Emily, Atkin. 'What Language Experts Find So Strange About Donald Trump.' ThinkProgress, 15 Sept. 2015, thinkprogress.org/what-language-experts-find-so-strange-about-donald-trump-2f067c20156e/.

# 34. TRUMP NICKNAMES OPPONENTS AND PEOPLE HE DOESN'T LIKE

Here are ten people Trump has famously insulted during debates and through Twitter, during campaign and post-campaign rallies, and in debates and the best explanations I could find.

| Person | Nickname/Insult | Explanation |
|---|---|---|
| Jeb Bush: Presumed Republican front-runner for the 2016 elections; former governor of Florida; son of President George H W Bush; brother of President George W Bush | 'Low-energy Jeb' | Jeb Bush presents himself as a low-key and thoughtful person. During his father's Presidency, he was known as the 'smart Bush son.' |
| Hillary Clinton: Democratic Presidential candidate in 2016; former Secretary of State; former Senator from New York; former First Lady | 'Crooked Hillary' | Trump built on a 20-year-plus campaign to discredit Hillary Clinton that began when her husband was President in the 1990s. Some people despised her for being an ambitious woman and she was accused of various crimes (and still continues to be). Clinton was the focus of many criminal investigations, all of which have exonerated her to date. |

| | | |
|---|---|---|
| James Comey, former director of the Federal Bureau of Investigation (FBI) | 'Nut Job' (leaked private conversation with Russia's two Sergeys, Foreign Minister Lavrov and Ambassador Kislyak) | Trump had just fired Comey after he refused to halt an investigation of Michael Flynn, the National Security advisor Trump appointed and had to fire a month later after Flynn admitted he had lied about meeting with Russian officials during the campaign. |
| Ted Cruz, Republican senator from Texas and primary opponent | 'Lyin' Ted' | This was a rebuttal Trump made during a Republican primary debate when Cruz brought up a *New York Times* interview with Trump on immigration. |
| Kim Jong Un, North Korean dictator | 'Rocket Man' | Kim launched many, many rockets in recent years, some of which exploded upon launch. As Trump tweeted out, this is 'very, very bad behavior.' |
| Marco Rubio, Republican senator from Florida and primary opponent | 'Little Marco' | Trump responded to Rubio's taunt about his small hands. |
| Bernie Sanders, Democratic Senator from Vermont and Democratic primary challenger to Hillary Clinton | 'Crazy Bernie' | Bernie Sanders does have a problem with his hair flying all over in windy weather, making him look, well, crazy. |

| Charles 'Chuck' Schumer, Democratic Senator from New York | 'Cryin' Chuck' | This was Trump's tweeted retort over Schumer's press conference calling for a special prosecutor to investigate Trump's firing of James Comey. |
|---|---|---|
| Jeff Sessions, Trump's Attorney General and former Senator from Alabama | 'Weak' | Trump tweeted this after Sessions recused himself from appointing a special prosecutor to look into Comey's firing. Instead, he had an Assistant Attorney General make the appointment. |
| Elizabeth Warren, Democratic senator from Massachusetts; Director of the US Consumer Protection Agency; Law Professor (University of Texas, University of Pennsylvania, Harvard University) | 'Pocahontas' | Warren's Senate opponent accused her of falsely claiming Native American heritage to help obtain a professorship at Harvard University. This has never been proven, but she was listed as a minority in a law directory. Pocahontas was a Powhatan woman and American folk hero known for saving the life of John Smith, an English settler her tribe intended to kill. |

## 35. TRUMP HAS BELONGED TO THREE DIFFERENT POLITICAL PARTIES OVER THE YEARS

Donald Trump has tried on at least three political parties for size:

In 1987, he registered as a Republican.
In 1999, he joined the Reform Party.
He was a Democrat 2001–2009.
In 2009, he became a Republican again.
He left the Republican Party in 2011; on his registration form, he ticked the box for 'I do not wish to enroll in a party.'
He rejoined the Republicans in 2012.

As a businessman, Trump donated to both the Democratic and Republican parties. Democrats generally dominate New York City politics, while both parties are competitive within New York State. He socialized with politicians from both, even inviting the Clintons to his 2005 wedding to Melania.

It's interesting to note that two of Trump's adult children—Eric and Ivanka—were not registered to vote in the New York Republican primary in 2016 although they had lived in the state all their lives except for four years at out-of-state universities. Clearly, this civic duty wasn't stressed as much as you would expect from a very public figure to his children.

The Reform Party is one of a handful of third parties in the United States. It was started by Ross Perot (b. 1930), a Texas billionaire who founded the IT company Electronic Data Systems (EDS), for his 1992 run for President. His campaign was largely viewed as a challenge to the Republican Party and President George H W Bush. Perot won nearly 19% of the popular vote but no electoral votes and the election went to Bill Clinton.

The Reform Party has backed Presidential candidates as far apart on the political spectrum as Pat Buchanan and Ralph Nader, candidates who split from the Republican and Democratic parties. In 1998, former pro wrestler Jesse Ventura ran and won as the

Reform candidate for governor of Minnesota. This no doubt caught Trump's attention.

In January 2000, Trump published *The America We Deserve*, in which he laid out his agenda alongside yet more autobiographical details (see Fact #72). 'Let's cut to the chase,' he wrote in the book's Introduction. 'Yes, I am considering a run for the presidency of the United States.'[1]

Oprah Winfrey was his ideal running mate, a choice he actually announced before the book was published. 'The political elites chortled,' he wrote. 'They just don't understand how many Americans respect and admire Oprah for her intelligence and caring. If I can't get Oprah, I'd like someone like her.'[1]

Trump repeated his offer in 2015, telling TV presenter George Stephanopoulos 'I think we'd win easily...I like Oprah. I mean, is that supposed to be a bad thing? I don't think so.'[2]

It's hard to imagine Winfrey, who had campaigned extensively for Barack Obama, winning over the right-wing mobs who dominated Trump rallies. Some people are urging her to consider a 2020 run as the 'anti-Trump.'

1 Trump, Donald. *The America We Deserve*. (Renaissance Books, 2000.)
2 Simon, Roger, et al. 'Trump Is No. 1, but Who's His No. 2?' *POLITICO*, 24 Feb. 2016, www.politico.com/story/2016/02/donald-trump-running-mate-pick-opinion-219692.

## 36. TRUMP PROMISES DONATIONS TO WHOMEVER OR WHATEVER HAS HIS ATTENTION

During his first meeting with G20 nations in July 2017, Trump said the US would provide $50 million to the Women Entrepreneurs Finance Initiative (We-Fi) World Bank fund that daughter Ivanka was championing at the time.

You might recall Trump's daughter Ivanka was very much present at these talks. She actually *sat* in her father's place after he 'stepped out' to do…we don't know what. She took her place with a group of elected world leaders who are normally replaced by senior officials (ministers, etc.) when they leave a meeting. As an assistant to the President, Ivanka clearly thought she was their equal, and according to the White House, she sat in during a part of the conversation that addressed women entrepreneurs in Africa.

Her father also pledged $639 million in humanitarian aid, half for areas hard-hit by famine: Somalia, South Sudan, Nigeria, and Yemen. If provided, it would continue the US' lead role in providing funds for famine relief. Of course, Trump cannot actually earmark these funds. That's a Congressional function. He can propose it in his budget.

As President, Trump submitted a budget blueprint to Congress a few months earlier, which, in fact, proposed to reduce nonmilitary foreign aid by nearly one-third. 'This budget expects the rest of the world to step up in some of the programs this country has been so generous in funding in the past,' Office of Management and Budget director Mick Mulvaney declared to a press conference. But all this happened before the G20 summit. Perhaps Trump was attempting to attack his own budget plan, which even many Republicans described as 'cruel.'

Certainly, Trump has a history of pledging funds and not following through on them.

In 1988, Trump joined a board charged with advising boxer Mike Tyson on business decisions. 'Anything I make from this position will go to charities fighting AIDS, cerebral palsy, multiple sclerosis, and helping the homeless,' Trump told reporters at a press conference in the Plaza Hotel, which he owned at the time.[1] An extensive investigation by three *BuzzFeed* reporters turned up no such donations, although Trump later said he wrote to Tyson to remind him to send his $2 million fee to his charity, the Donald J. Trump Foundation. *BuzzFeed* found no deposit to the foundation and since Trump won't release his tax records, it isn't possible to check to see he followed up on donation pledges.[2]

Trump supposedly donated proceeds from the Trump Vodka brand, which is still sold in a few places, to the Walter Reed Society that supports the Walter Reed Army Medical Center just outside Washington DC. The society told *BuzzFeed* it only received a few hundred dollars.[2]

In 2007, Trump stated he would donate $100,000 to Fisher House, a charity that supports hospitalized veterans. But the donation actually came from Trump's foundation, to which he had donated just $35,000 that year. Other businesses like Wrestlemania, which donated $4 million to it that year, have provided the bulk of the foundation's support.[2]

1 Rogers, Thomas. 'Tyson Welcomes Trump to Corner.' *The New York Times*, 11 July 1988, www.nytimes.com/1988/07/12/sports/tyson-welcomes-trump-to-corner.html.
2 Andrew Kaczynski, Christopher Massie, Nathan McDermott. 'Trump Promised Millions To Charity, But Gave Little To His Own Foundation.' *BuzzFeed*, https://goo.gl/3z2gdt.

## 37. THE 'LYING MEDIA' OFTEN FORCES TRUMP TO HONOR HIS CHARITY PLEDGES

During the Presidential campaign, Trump pledged $1 million to a veterans' charity but didn't actually pay up until the 'lying media' kept pressing him on it.

This reluctance to follow up on donations wasn't new. According to *The Atlantic*, Trump promised some $8.5 million in donations during the preceding 15 years.[1] (Not a lot for a billionaire, right?) But public records show he donated just $2.8 million to his own foundation, which in turn gave away about one-third of this amount. Trump's last donation to his own foundation came in 2008, which the New York State Attorney General's Office shut down in 2013.

Where did some of this money go? $258,000 was used to settle legal problems related to a pledge he made on his television show *The Apprentice*, and $20,000 went to buy a portrait of Trump that hangs in his Florida golf resort.[1]

Trump claims he gives away millions of dollars 'privately,' but there is no way to confirm this since he steadfastly refuses to release his income taxes for public view, something all other presidential candidates have done.

The Eric Trump Foundation is featured on the website for Trump.com. Founded in 2006, it raises money for St. Jude Children's Research Hospital, a leading pediatric treatment and research hospital that focuses on catastrophic diseases. Ironically, the late actor and comedian Danny Thomas, born Amos Muzyad Yakhoob Kairouz in Deerfield, Michigan to Lebanese immigrants, founded St. Jude. Lebanon is among the nations Trump has singled out for an immigration ban.

---

1 Friedersdorf, Conor. 'Donald Trump's False Bragging About His Charitable Giving.' *The Atlantic*, 28 Dec. 2016, www.theatlantic.com/politics/archive/2016/12/donald-trumps-mendacious-bragging-about-his-charitable-giving/511703/.

# 38. TRUMP IS THE 'LEAST RACIST' PERSON YOU'LL MEET

Long before the 2016 Iowa Caucus—the first step to win delegates for a party's nomination for President—Trump had been establishing his persona. *The Chicago Tribune* highlighted a few that really show the extent of Trump's vanity:

'I'm like, a really smart person.' He's also tweeted that his IQ is one of the 'highest.'
'I have the world's greatest memory.'
'I'm self-funding my campaign.' There's always been a 'donate' button on his campaign websites.
'I'm probably the least racist person on Earth.'[1]

That last one is so over-the-top I have to wonder if he *is* being ironic after all.

Trump's family has a history of casual, if not outright, racism toward blacks starting with his father's arrest during a Ku Klux Klan rally discussed in Fact #17, which covers the US Government's lawsuit against the Trumps for discriminating against black applicants to rent Trump-owned flats.

Trump has never apologized for his 1989 campaign to reinstate the death penalty in New York for the so-called Central Park Five, who were black and Latino. (See Fact #39 below.) Trump placed full-page adverts in all the major New York papers demanding the death penalty for the five—before they were even tried.

In 1992, The Trump Plaza and Casino was fined $200,000 for removing a black dealer from a table because a patron—reportedly a member of John Gotti's crime family—objected to his presence. An appeals court upheld the fine. In September 2017, black employees at the steakhouse in Trump's new hotel in Washington, DC sued after being repeatedly assigned to lower-paying shifts

---

1 Kessler, Glenn. 'Donald Trump's Myths about Himself.' *Chicago Tribune*, 1 Feb. 2016, www.chicagotribune.com/news/nationworld/ct-donald-trump-myths-20160128-story.html.

after the 2016 election. One says a white employee told him, 'This is white America time, you need to get used to it.'[2]

Trump has never apologized for characterizing Mexicans as 'criminals,' 'drug dealers' and 'rapists,' the motivation behind his call to build a 'big, beautiful wall' along the US-Mexico border.

Trump has repeatedly called for a 'Muslim ban' during his candidacy and since his election has signed Executive Orders to ban Muslims from several countries the State Department says sponsors terrorism or tolerates terrorists—but not Saudi Arabia where he has business interests, and where most of the 9/11 terrorists came from.

At a rally the night before the South Carolina primary, Trump told the crowd a discredited story about US General John Pershing. The story says Pershing's troops rounded up Muslim terrorists in the Philippines in the early 1900s and killed them with bullets dipped in pigs' blood. Trump's campaign manager at the time, Corey Lewanowski, was asked why Trump used a patently false story and answered, 'This is toughness...Look, it's an analogy.'[3]

In December 2015, Trump told a group of Jewish Republicans that he was 'a negotiator like you folks.'[1] As the father of a Jewish convert (Ivanka) and a native of New York City, it's nearly impossible not to comprehend the offensive nature of such a comment.

2  Hill, Zahara. 'Black Employees Of Trump International Hotel File Racial Discrimination Suit.' *Ebony*, 23 Sept. 2017, https://goo.gl/3CrHfX.

3  Kranish and Fischer, *Trump Revealed*, 2016

# 39. TRUMP ADVOCATED THE DEATH PENALTY FOR DEFENDANTS LATER FOUND INNOCENT

Trump is an enthusiastic supporter of the death penalty. In 1989, he paid about $80,000 for full-page advertisements in all four New York City daily newspapers to demand the death penalty for five teenagers who had been arrested two weeks earlier for a horrific rape in Central Park that nearly killed its victim, a young white woman.

Not only did this serve to inflame a tense racial situation, it prejudiced potential jurors for a trial. Then Trump told a TV reporter he 'would love to be a well-educated black because they have an actual advantage.'[1]

Four of the teenagers were black and one was Latino. Four confessed to the crime after intensive questioning over many hours. Three did not have attorneys or parents present because police believed they were over age 16; one was in fact younger and questioning ended once his mother arrived. He was the only one who did not tape a confession.

Two trials were held in 1990 in which the defendants argued they signed confessions under duress, were too young to understand the nature of the charges, or were coerced. Three were found guilty on all charges except attempted murder in the first trial, and the other two were found guilty of all charges including attempted murder in the second one.

The US Constitution prohibits self-incrimination under duress, which explains the confessions because it turns out, the boys—dubbed The Central Park Five—were in fact innocent. Why would anyone confess to a crime he didn't commit? Because police questioning is meant to elicit confessions. The defendants in this case were also denied food, water, and sleep for 45 hours. Few adults, let alone teenagers, can stand up to this.

DNA testing was too new to be reliable. Jurors later said they didn't put too much faith in the confessions because they were so

---

1 Michael D'Antonio, *Never Enough*, 2015.

uneven and filled with holes, but were moved by physical evidence from the crime scene.

In 2002, a convicted serial rapist and murderer declared he committed the rape. He provided a detailed account and his DNA, which matched evidence saved from the crime scene. The New York Supreme Court overturned all the convictions, although all the defendants had served their full terms. Later, they accepted a settlement from the city.

Donald Trump never apologized or acknowledged the Central Park Five's proven innocence. Instead, he sticks to his conviction that since they were in Central Park that night, they must have been up to something. He insists that they were behind other attacks that went on the same night, although there is no evidence for any of this either.

The exonerated five believe Trump's grandstanding in the New York press helped seal their fate. 'He was literally like the fire starter, he lit the match,' says Yusef Salaam, who was 15 at the time of his arrest and didn't confess to the crime.[2]

It's one thing to be outraged by crime, but quite another to target your rage at the wrong people.

---

2 @NewDay. 'One of the falsely accused 'Central Park Five' speaks out: Donald Trump 'was the fire starter, he lit the match." *Twitter*, 6 Oct. 2016, https://twitter.com/NewDay/status/784001121505382400

# 40. HATE CRIMES IN THE US GREW WITH TRUMP'S POPULARITY

The 2016 campaign appears to have encouraged more hate crimes and expressions of racial and ethnic prejudice in the US.

Hate speech had already been rising and edged into Republican politics after Barack Obama's election. Calls came for Obama's assassination came from people like aging rocker Ted Nugent, an NRA board member and a regular performer at Republican campaign events. Republican gubernatorial candidates like Trump pal Carl Paladino sent around emails with extraordinarily offensive video clips and photos. It became the new norm in too many Republican circles as moderates looked the other way or even excused or explained away such behavior.

But with Trump's campaign and embrace of unapologetic racists, years of bottled-up racial, ethnic, and gender hatred exploded on social media, often triggered by well-known code words Trump uttered at rallies. (Examples: 'the wall that Mexico will pay for,' 'Muslim bans,' and of course, the false 'birther' claims about Obama's origins he clung to until September 2016.)

The Southern Poverty Law Center, a nonprofit organization that tracks hate crimes and litigates on civil rights issues, counted 1,094 incidents of hate during the first month after Trump's election, and 900 in the ten days following it.[1] While the number of hate crimes dropped in the months that followed, their severity rose and included murders. Two men were stabbed to death after coming to assist two Muslim girls being harassed on public transit in Portland, Oregon, in February 2017. Two Indian-born engineers were shot to death in a restaurant Olathe, Kansas, also in February. In May 2017, a black student days away from graduating from Maryland's Bowie State University was stabbed to death while waiting for a ride back to campus from the University of Maryland. The killer was a member of a Facebook

---

1 'Ten Days After: Harassment and Intimidation in the Aftermath of the Election.' Southern Poverty Law Center, 9 November 2016, www.splcenter.org/20161129/ten-days-after-harassment-and-intimidation-aftermath-election.

group called 'Alt-Reich Nation.' In August 2017, a self-professed admirer of Nazis rammed a car into a crowd of people peacefully protesting an 'alt-right' rally in Charlottesville, Virginia, killing one woman.[1]

According to the Center for the Study of Hate and Extremism at California State University, San Bernardino, hate crimes rose substantially in 2016 compared to 2015. They rose 23% in nine metropolitan areas it studied. They went up 62% in Washington, DC and 24% in New York City. Anti-Semitic crimes against Jewish groups rose 189% during a single three-month period in 2015 compared to one year earlier.[2]

A September 2017 Center report on vetted police data from over 40 US cities back up the Southern Poverty Law Center data. Here are some of its findings:

Hate crimes rose 5% between 2015 and 2016 across America, with dramatic spikes in large cities.
There were notable increases in hate crimes around the election.
Blacks continued to be the group most targeted for hate crimes.
Hate crimes against GLBT were particularly dramatic in New York City, Chicago, Phoenix, Seattle, Washington, DC, and San Francisco.

The Center predicts that once all statistics are complied, hate crimes will have surpassed 6,000 in 2016 for the first time ever.[2]

---

2 Levin, Brian. *Hate Crimes Rise in Major American Localities in 2016*. California State University, San Bernardino, Center for the Study of Hate and Extremism, https://csbs.csusb.edu/sites/csusb_csbs/files/Levin%20 DOJ%20Summit%202.pdf.

# 41. IN CASE YOU HAVEN'T HEARD, TRUMP HAD A VERY, VERY POPULAR TELEVISION SHOW

Trump's popularity grew during the run of his television show *The Apprentice* from 2004 through 2007. A later show, *Celebrity Apprentice*, ran from 2007 to 2017.

The original *Apprentice* was actually a pretty good show. It pegged two teams of entrepreneurs simultaneously to work cooperatively and against one another on various projects. Trump would famously fire someone on the losing team each week, usually the team leader, with his signature phrase 'you're fired!' Fired contestants often appeared on the network's news show the following morning.

At the end of each season, two people would square off, with Trump declaring to the winner 'you're hired!' Winners would get a job for one year with The Trump Organization, at a salary of $250,000. Everyone in the UK knows that Lord Sugar still does the firing. The show is or was franchised all over the world. (In Estonia it was called *Mantlipärija*, which seems to have something to do with taking up a mantle.)

*The Apprentice* won the Primetime Emmy Award in 2004 and 2005 for Outstanding Reality-Competition Program. Trump was nominated for a Teen Choice Award for Variety TV Star-Male in 2004.

*The Apprentice* gave Trump his fiercest obsession: ratings. Sam Solovey, a first-season contestant says he found Trump slumped and dejected the day he learned that *The Apprentice* had been beaten in the ratings.[1]

Solovey went on to work with The Trump Organization to help boost the show's ratings and the Trump brand. 'He is obsessed with metrics, polls and data,' he told biographers Kranish and Fisher.[1]

NBC fired Trump as the *Celebrity Apprentice* host in 2015 for his 'derogatory' statements about immigrants and ended televising his beauty pageants as well.

*The New Celebrity Apprentice* ran for a few weeks in early 2017, with Arnold Schwarzenegger as host.

---

1 Kranish and Fisher, *Trump Revealed*, 2016.

## 42. TRUMP HAS BEEN AS OBSESSED WITH A COMEDIENNE AS HE HAS WITH HILLARY

Whenever Trump is having a slow news day, or needs to distract the nation from various investigations that involve him, his family, or his Administration, he attacks comedienne Rosie O'Donnell or more recently, Hillary Clinton.

It's kind of weird, because both women have been guests at Donald's weddings. Rosie was at Wedding Number Two to Marla 'The Other Woman' Maples in 1993 while the Clintons famously attended Wedding Number Three to Melania in 2005.

The O'Donnell/Trump feud seems to go back to late 2006 and early 2007 and it's about, of course, a beauty queen. In 2006, Trump owned the Miss USA and Miss Teen USA beauty pageants. That year, Tara Conner, the reigning Miss USA, was discovered to have used drugs, engaged in underage drinking, and most shockingly, sneaked men into her suite at Trump Place. She also publicly snogged with Miss Teen USA.

Somewhat surprisingly, Trump refused to fire her. 'I've always been a believer in second chances,' he said.[1] He may have also been thinking of his later brother Freddy, who died from the effects of alcoholism. Conner entered rehab and has since spoken about her struggle with substance abuse.

It's odd to think someone is less forgiving than Donald Trump, but Rosie O'Donnell apparently can be. The day after Trump announced he wasn't going to fire Conner, O'Donnell used her platform on the popular chat show *The View* to criticize the decision. Then she attacked Trump for not being a 'self-made man' and a 'snake-oil salesman' who 'left his first wife—had an affair... [has] the moral compass of a 20-year old.'[2]

1 'Trump Decides Not to Fire Miss USA Tara Conner.' Fox News, 19 Dec. 2006, www.foxnews.com/story/2006/12/19/trump-decides-not-to-fire-miss-usa-tara-conner.html.

2 Zaru, Deena. 'The Donald Trump-Rosie O'Donnell Feud: A Timeline.' CNN, 14 Aug. 2017, www.cnn.com/201/08/14/politics/donald-trump-rosie-odonnell-feud/index.html.

Remember, she had attended Trump's wedding to Marla Maples, who carried on an affair with Trump while he was still married to Ivana.

Trump fought back via *People*, a popular and somewhat respectable tabloid magazine and called O'Donnell 'a woman out of control' and his favorite insult, 'a loser.'[2]

Several months later, O'Donnell left *The View* after a heated argument with its token conservative, Elisabeth Hasselbeck, over the US role in the Iraq war. Trump, who had criticized both women in the press—he told the TV show *Extra* that Hasselbeck is 'one of the dumber people in television'—sort of defended O'Donnell. 'On this one I think Rosie should win...because to justify the war in Iraq—only an imbecile could do that.'

Things were pretty quiet on the Trump–O'Donnell front until later 2011 when O'Donnell announced her engagement to her girlfriend. By then, Trump had been active on Twitter for about two years and used the medium to broadcast his feelings on the engagement.

'I feel sorry for Rosie's new partner in love whose parents are devastated at the thought of their daughter being @Rosie—a true loser.'

Rosie's reply: '@realDonaldTrump – wow u r an ass in every way.'

## 43. TRUMP REMAINED OBSESSED WITH ROSIE DURING THE 2016 CAMPAIGN1

In 2012, Trump tweeted insults about Cher, Mitt Romney—at the time, the Republican nominee for President—and O'Donnell in a single tweet. Think about it: three people mocked in just 140 characters!

Romney, who denounced Trump during the 2016 campaign, nevertheless groveled to him after he won the Presidential race, hoping to be named Secretary of Something, possibly State. That position, of course, went to ExxonMobil chairman Rex Tillerson.

Later in 2012, when O'Donnell suffered a heart attack, Trump tweeted his hope that she would 'get better fast. I'm starting to miss you!'

Rosie replied, 'i must admit ur post was a bit of a shock...r u trying to kill me xx.'

There was some back-and-forth tweeting in 2014 after O'Donnell announced she had lost 50 pounds via weight loss surgery and told an American Heart Association gathering that her weight gain was due to her neglecting her health. Trump tweeted about a month later that O'Donnell had previously shamed another celebrity who also had weight loss surgery. O'Donnell's reply: 'Donald—go away.'

Things really went into overdrive later that year when O'Donnell returned to *The View*. In an interview with *People*, she commented that the criticism she received from Trump was the 'most bullying I ever experienced in my life, including as a child. It was national, and it was sanctioned socially. Whether I deserved it is up to your own interpretation.'

Trump tweeted back, '@Rosie—no offense, and good luck on the show, but remember, you started it!'

O'Donnell left The *View* a second time after just a year, explaining that stress from the show and her breakup with her wife wasn't healthy for a heart attack survivor. Trump told *ENews* that he 'likes the show a lot, but let's face it, Rosie is a loser.'

Things were pretty quiet on the Rosie front for a few months after Trump took office—after all, there was that Russia investigation that should have been about Hillary Clinton's emails, or opposition research, or her husband's infidelities—until May. Rose did actually start it. She responded to a Trump tweet stating 'there is no evidence of collusion w/Russia and Trump.' Rosie tweeted: 'RESIGN YOU PATEHTIC (sic) MORONIC SPOILED RICH PRICK.'

Apparently, this escaped Trump's attention. Instead, he responded a few days later to a December 20 2016 tweet from Rosie that said 'FIRE COMEY.' Trump re-tweeted this with the comment, 'We finally agree on something Rosie.'

Actually, O'Donnell had probably been voicing anger at James Comey, who was believed in some circles to have swung the election to Trump by re-opening an investigation into Hillary Clinton's emails a few days earlier. (Certainly, Hillary believes this is the case.) As the January 20 Inauguration Day neared, plenty of Americans were in a state of panic and the Comey re-re-reinvestigation was re-re-revisited in the press.

Five months later,Trump fired Comey for entirely different reasons (see Fact #85).

1 Deena Zaru, CNN, 2017.

# 44. TRUMP LIKES MUSIC BY MUSICIANS WHO WANT NOTHING TO DO WITH HIM

Trump is a fan of Sir Elton John, according to *Business Insider*.[1] 'Rocket Man' and 'Tiny Dancer' are two songs played at some of his rallies. But the love was not returned. Elton told *The Guardian* that he'd met Donald Trump. While 'he was very nice to me, it's nothing personal,' their political views are quite different. 'I'm not a Republican in a million years. Why not ask Ted f——g Nugent?'[2]

Sir Elton joined an impressive list of pop stars who told The Donald to stop playing their music at his rallies:[3]

Adele objected to the campaign using 'Rolling in the Deep' to warm up the crowds.

Neil Young protested when 'Rockin' in the Free World' was used at Trump's rally to announce his candidacy.

Twisted Sister rescinded an earlier agreement to let the campaign use 'We're Not Gonna Take It' (not the same as The Who's song from *Tommy*). 'I had to ask him to stop using the song,' lead singer Dee Snider told *Billboard*. He had to tell Trump that he 'didn't realize some of the things you were going to represent—the wall, banning Muslims. I can't get behind some of those things.' Trump was 'OK' about dropping the song.

The Rolling Stones' 'Start Me Up' was played after Trump's acceptance speech at the Republican convention. 'The Rolling Stones have never given permission to the Trump campaign to use

1 Tani, Maxwell. 'The Songs That Donald Trump Rallies Blast to Pump up Supporters.' *Business Insider*, 9 Jan. 2016, www.businessinsider.com/donald-trump-rally-songs-2015-12/#rocket-man--elton-john-1.
2 Petridis, Alexis. 'Elton John: 'Our Kids Aren't Stuck in a Mansion. We Go to Pizza Hut'.' *The Guardian*, 7 Feb. 2016, www.theguardian.com/music/2016/feb/07/elton-john-i-really-hate-the-cult-of-celebrity.
3 Carissimo, Justin. 'A List of Musicians Who Want Donald Trump to Stop Playing Their Music.' *The Independent*, 22 July 2016, www.independent.co.uk/news/world/americas/us-elections/musicians-who-want-donald-trump-to-stop-playing-their-music-a7151171.html.

their songs and have requested they cease all use immediately,' a spokesperson told *Time*.[4]

Before you say, oh please, it's not like he chooses the songs—he did. Ryan Lizza reported in *The New Yorker* in February 2016 that Trump created song lists to be played for fifty minutes before he took to the stage at each rally. The list included Stones hits like 'Brown Sugar' and 'Sympathy for the Devil.' 'The more inappropriate [a song is] for a political event, the better,' a volunteer told Lizza.[5]

Neil Young has his own strange history with Trump. The two had met to discuss financing for Young's music streaming service Pono a few months before Trump announced his candidacy for President. Young wasn't happy with Trump using 'Rockin' the Free World' and sent his representatives to tell the campaign to stop. But the Trump campaign had paid the required royalty fee to use the song. Trump tweeted an undated photo of the two shaking hands after the Pono meeting and called Young 'a total hypocrite.' A follow-up tweet said he 'Didn't love it [the song] anyway.'

At times, Young has said he would have been OK with the song being used if he'd been asked for permission—which isn't required. He posted a clip of himself playing the song, in which he repeatedly shouts 'f—k you Donald Trump' on his Facebook page. You can see it here: https://www.facebook.com/NeilYoung/videos/10156963043720317/

4 Beckwith, Ronald Teague. 'Donald Trump: Rolling Stones Ask Him to Stop Using Music.' *Time*, 4 May 2016, time.com/4318122/donald-trump-rolling-stones-music-playlist-rally/.

5 Lizza, Ryan. 'On the Road with Trump and Cruz.' *The New Yorker*, 19 June 2017, www.newyorker.com/magazine/2016/02/01/the-duel-faceoff-ryan-lizza.

# 45. HE'S *DOCTOR* TRUMP, LOSER!

Trump has been awarded six honorary degrees from five universities, with one university officially stripping him of the honor in 2015.

Robert Gordon University in Aberdeen gave him an honorary Doctor of Business Administration in 2010 as he prepared to build the 'world's greatest golf course' at Menie in Aberdeenshire. Not everyone was pleased; the Tripping Up Trump campaign said in a statement that 'the only award Donald Trump is worthy of is an Asbo.'

The university stripped him of the degree in December 2015 after the President-Elect called for a ban on Muslims entering the US. He also lost his position as a business ambassador for Scotland, to which then-First Minister Jack McConnell had appointed him in 2006.

Liberty University, a very conservative Christian university in Lynchburg, Virginia, has given Trump two honorary doctorates. It awarded him a doctorate of business in 2012 and gave him an honorary law degree during its commencement ceremony in May 2017. In response, a group of Liberty alumni created a private Facebook page called 'Return Your Diploma to LU.' Within a day, it had nearly 300 members including 50 who planned to do just that. (Some of them apparently joined because they were reporting on the activity.)

Lehigh University in Bethlehem, Pennsylvania, awarded Trump an honorary doctorate of laws in 1988. Although more than 30,000 people signed a petition to revoke the degree, Lehigh's Board voted to take no action on it at its October 2017 meeting.

Wagner College in Staten Island, New York, gave him an honorary doctorate of humane letters in 2012.

# 46. TRUMP HAS SOME WEIRD IDEAS ABOUT DISEASE

Perhaps Trump thinks these honorary doctorates infuse him with medical expertise, because he certainly isn't shy about sharing his medical opinions on topics like the causes of disease.

He has tweeted many times in support of the palpably false link between vaccines and autism, a claim that's been studied for years at considerable expense and thoroughly debunked. This one is on you, Brits. The vaccine debate started when English physician Andrew Wakefield published an article in *The Lancet* that used falsified data to show a link between receiving vaccines and developing autism. *The Lancet* had to retract the study and Wakefield lost his license. He now lives in Texas, where he has been denied a medical license.

That hasn't stopped him and an army of anti-vaxxers from sounding alarms that are strangely reminiscent of the uproar that forced thousands of pet dogs into quarantine back in the 1980s and 1990s.

There is no doubt that autism diagnoses have risen in Western nations. One reason could be the lack of solid guidelines. It is also diagnosed via observation, not physical criteria like blood counts or brain scans, so diagnostics are highly subjective. But the link to vaccines has been thoroughly disproven.

Vaccines, on the other hand, have eliminated diseases that used to routinely cause disabilities and deaths. I remember growing up around adults with shrunken limbs caused by polio. Like many people of our generation, my siblings and I had chicken pox; years later, my eldest brother nearly lost an eye to shingles, which surfaces *only* in people who've had chicken pox. Other diseases that used to cause childhood disabilities and even deaths we thought vaccines had eliminated like measles and pertussis have returned because people aren't vaccinating their children.

Equally alarming is Trump's belief that asbestos, which has been known for years to be the only cause for the deadly disease mesothelioma, is '100% safe.' He's said this for years. In his book *The Art of the Comeback*, he says asbestos is an 'incredible fireproofing material' that was banned by pressure from 'the mob.' Organized crime, he says, own the companies that provide asbestos removal. So mesothelioma is a conspiracy.

Except it's not. Major scientific bodies including the World Health Organization, the British Lung Foundation, and the US National Institute for Occupational Safety and Health are just a few that have concluded without any doubt that exposure to asbestos causes mesothelioma.

Asbestos is still used in the US, where in spite of government-issued safety guidelines for handling it, 15,000 Americans who have been exposed to it die each year. This number includes workers who install it, car mechanics (it's used in manufacturing brakes) and incredibly, teachers who are exposed to asbestos crumbling off ceilings and walls in aging public schools.

Finally, Trump's anti-science outlook has serious consequences for research into disease prevention and treatment. By withdrawing from the Paris Agreement and installing a virulent climate change denier as head of the US Environmental Protection Administration, he's enabling US industries to end their efforts to reduce their carbon footprint and safely dispose of toxins. At the same time, he's ripping away funds from research into health and the environment in exchange for tax breaks for those same companies.

# 47. TRUMP IS OBSESSED WITH OTHER PEOPLE'S WEIGHT

Nothing obsesses Trump more than other people's weight. It doesn't matter if the person is a spouse, beauty pageant winner, mouthy television personality, or even someone who may not exist: if Trump perceives that person is fat, he or she will be shamed on Twitter and other venues.

Actress and comedienne Rosie O'Donnell was Trump's favorite target for several years before she had gastric sleeve surgery following a heart attack. Since then, Trump has mostly stuck to tweeting more generic insults about her.

As Hillary Clinton asserted during a debate that Trump had called women 'fat pigs' and other names, Trump stalked around the stage muttering 'only Rosie O'Donnell' into his microphone.

Clinton pointed out that Trump had called the 1996 Miss Universe, Alicia Machado, 'Miss Piggy' after she had gained weight during the year of her 'reign.' (Trump owned the Miss Universe pageant at the time.) Trump had denied this in the past, but Machado and others confirmed it.[1]

This was also the same debate where Trump's response to a question about cybercrime and a security breach at the Democratic National Headquarters was to speculate that the hacker 'could be somebody sitting on their bed that weighs 400 pounds.' Tech people were mostly amused by the comment. '#400poundhacker' briefly trended on Twitter, where one person enthused it would be 'an awesome name for a band.'

Women who worked in executive positions for the Trump Organization were subjected to comments about their weight. Barbara Res, who was head of construction in the 1980s (an unusual position for a woman to have at that time) told *The New York Times* that Trump once hinted to her that she needed to lose weight by commenting 'you like your candy.'[1]

---

1 Twohey, Michael Barbaro and Megan. 'Crossing the Line: How Donald Trump Behaved With Women in Private.' *The New York Times*, 14 May 2016, www.nytimes.com/2016/05/15/us/politics/donald-trump-women.html?_r=0.

Not all women were annoyed to listen to observations about their weight. Louise Sunshine, who was a vice president at the Trump Organization, told *The Times* that she regarded such observations as 'friendly encouragement.' Sunshine, who now heads her own real estate company, also told the PBS show *Frontline* that she puts in 'imaginary earplugs' when Trump says things she doesn't like or want to hear. It's certainly an original coping strategy.

Even celebrities don't escape Trump's weight obsession. He wanted to fire Khloé Kardashian, of the family who invented fame without actually doing anything, from *Celebrity Apprentice* because she was 'a fat piglet.' He also called her sister Kim 'fat' when she was actually pregnant. (Kim may have been 'the hot one' he said he really wanted on the show.)[2]

Melania hasn't escaped Trump's obsession with weight, either. Several publications reported that Trump agreed to her pregnancy when she promised to lose all the baby weight. A *New York Post* columnist, Andrea Peyser, wrote about visiting Melania a couple of months after Barron was born in 2006. She complimented her on how good she looked 'aboard five-inch stilettos' and for losing 'all' the baby weight. 'Almost all,' hubby Donald corrected her. Melania, Peyser wrote, ignored this jibe.[3]

Donald Trump in 100 Facts

2 Spargo, Chris. "I Find It Really Cruel': Khloé Kardashian Slams 'Shady' Donald Trump and Says He Is Not Fit to Run the Country after Report That He Called Her a 'Fat Piglet' and 'Ugly'." *Daily Mail Online*, 18 Oct. 2016, www.dailymail.co.uk/news/article-3848382/I-really-cruel-Khloe-Kardashian-slams-shady-Donald-Trump-says-not-fit-run-country-report-called-fat-piglet-ugly.html.

3 Peyser, Andrea. 'I Can No Longer Justify Calling Myself a Trump Supporter.' *New York Post*, 7 Aug. 2016, www.gopbriefingroom.com/index.php?topic=219662.0.

## 48. TRUMP ONCE RECOMMENDED A ONE-TIME 'MASSIVE' TAX ON THE RICH TO WIPE OUT THE NATIONAL DEBT

Way back in the dying days of the 20th century, CNN (AKA 'Fake News') reported that 'billionaire businessman' Donald Trump said the United States could retire its debt by levying a 14.25% one-time 'net worth tax' on all people and trusts worth over $10 million.In fact, he proposed this in an economic plan he released as he mulled over a potential run for the Presidency in 2000.

'The plan I am proposing today does not involve smoke and mirrors, phony numbers, financial gimmicks, or the usual economic chicanery you usually find in Disneyland-on-the-Potomac,' he told CNN in November 1999. Just one percent of Americans 'who control 90% of the wealth in this country,' would be affected by the plan.

'Personally, this plan would cost me hundreds of millions of dollars, but in all honesty, it's worth it,' Trump said, because it would save the US $200 billion each year in interest payments. If elected, he would uset those savings for middle class tax cuts and social security for retired people over 65.[1]

So where did this guy go?

The proposals Trump has championed during his first year in office are a direct hit to the health and welfare of middle income Americans he championed until he took office. Even his top economic advisor admitted that his tax reform plan won't help middle-class Americans and some may actually see their taxes go up.[2]

1 Hirschkorn, Phil. 'Trump Proposes Massive One-Time Tax on the Rich.' CNN, 9 Nov. 1999, www.cnn.com/ALLPOLITICS/stories/1999/11/09/trump.rich/index.html?_s=PM%3AALLPOLITICS.
2 Winsor, Morgan. 'Trump Adviser 'Can't Guarantee' Taxes Won't Go up for Middle Class.' ABC News, 28 Sept. 2017, abcnews.go.com/Politics/trump-adviser-guarantee-taxes-middle-class/story?id=50149729.

# 49. TRUMP IS DISRESPECTFUL TOWARDS WOMEN

Donald Trump does not respect women. His CV is filled with commentary about women based on their appearances and expressing horror over things that are part of being female.

Perhaps his best-known comment from the 2016 campaign came from the first televised Republican debate that aired on the Fox News channel. One of the moderators, Megyn Kelly, asked Trump about his temperament given his past description of women he dislikes: 'you call them fat pigs, dogs, slobs, and disgusting animals.' As usual, Trump said he was only speaking of Rosie O'Donnell; Kelly replied that he'd used this language with other women as well.

Trump answered that the country's real problem was being 'politically correct,' to thunderous applause from the Fox audience. 'What I say is what I say…and if you don't like it, I'm sorry, I've been very nice to you, although I could probably maybe not…'[1]

The following day, Trump described Kelly as crazed, with 'blood coming out of her eyes, blood coming out of her whatever.'[2] A fascinating choice of words.

Normal biological functions really freak him out. In 2011, he called an attorney who was part of a team deposing him 'disgusting' because she requested a break to pump milk for her infant. Trump's lawyers objected, so she took out a breast pump from her bag to illustrate the urgency. At that point, the attorney says, Trump had 'a meltdown.' When the story broke in 2015, Trump charged that the attorney wanted to pump 'in front of

---

1 'Donald Trump and Megyn Kelly go back and forth at the Fox News GOP Debate,' *YouTube*, uploaded by Fox News Insider, 6 Aug. 2015, https://www.youtube.com/watch?v=1Y9_LJj7A68.

2 Yan, Holly. 'Trump Draws Outrage after Megyn Kelly Remarks – CNNPolitics.' *CNN*, 8 Aug. 2015, www.cnn.com/2015/08/08/politics/donald-trump-cnn-megyn-kelly-comment/index.html.

me.' None of the others in the room recall this at all, just that she needed to leave the room.[3]

Women who appeared on *The Apprentice* were subject to humiliating treatment such as boardroom discussions about their appearance, one told *The New York Times*, and being rated as 'hot' or 'not hot.'

During a *Celebrity Apprentice* boardroom meeting in 2010, contestant and team lead Bret Michaels explained that fellow contestant Brande Roderick, a former Playboy model, came 'on her knees' to beg him not to recommend her firing. Trump responded that 'it must be a pretty picture' to see her on her knees. At least one of the advisors, Piers Morgan, laughed at the comment; which won't surprise many in the UK.[4]

In 2011, *New York Times* columnist and satirist Gail Collins recalled the time she referred to Trump as a 'financially embattled thousandaire.' He responded by sending her a copy of the column with her picture circled and 'The Face of a Dog!' written over it.

Collins went on to lampoon Trump and *The Apprentice*, noting that he had 'the moral fortitude to tell Dionne Warwick she is fired.' (I remember that season, and Warwick was hilarious as the very quintessence of a jaded employee.) It's noteworthy that Collins ended her column by noting that Trump, then in the throes of 'Birthergate,' released a copy of his own birth certificate. 'Now,' she ended, 'let's try asking to see his tax returns.'[5]

---

3 Barbaro, Michael. 'Donald Trump Calls Lawyer in Breast-Pump Incident a 'Horrible Person'. *The New York Times*, 29 July 2015, www.nytimes.com/politics/first-draft/2015/07/29/donald-trump-calls-lawyer-in-breast-pump-incident-a-horrible-person/

4 'Donald Trump tells Brande Roderick being on her knees is a pretty picture.' YouTube, uploaded by Cowger Nation, 16 Aug. 2015, https://www.youtube.com/watch?v=n7NDpHfXTCI.

5 Collins, Gail. 'Opinion | Donald Trump Gets Weirder.' *The New York Times*, 1 Apr. 2011, www.nytimes.com/2011/04/02/opinion/02collins.html.

# 50. TRUMP DONATES HIS PRESIDENTIAL SALARY

Trump has stuck to a campaign pledge to donate his Presidential salary, which amounts to $400,000 per year. He donated his first-quarter salary of about $78,000 to the National Park Service (NPS), which can use all the help it can get since Trump wants to reduce its budget by 18%.

According to NPS staff, the budget calls for personnel reductions severe enough that it will be forced to close campgrounds and other facilities at a time when more people than ever visit the nation's national parks. Natural resource projects would face the most impacts with a cut of nearly 25%. The reason? Trump wants to privatize services in national parks. 'I don't want to be in the business of running campgrounds,' Interior Secretary Ryan Zinke told *The Hill*.[1]

But Trump's donation went to restoring two projects at the Antietam National Battlefield in Maryland. Antietam is the site where Robert E. Lee surrendered the Confederate army to General (and later President) Ulysses S. Grant. 'I can find no better investment than our battlefields,' Zinke told NPS employees at Antietam, some of whom will soon lose their jobs.[2]

Trump's second quarter salary of $100,000 went to the Department of Education, which said it would use it to host a STEM (science, technology, engineering and mathematics) camp. There have not been any details about the camp itself.

The proposed budget for education would be reduced by 13.5%, and include enormous reductions to financial aid for university students and those seeking post-high school training.[3]

1 Cama, Timothy. 'Companies Push Trump to Outsource Work in National Parks.' *The Hill*, 30 June 2017, thehill.com/policy/energy-environment/340181-hospitality-industry-pushes-trump-for-bigger-role-in-national-parks.
2 Cama, Timothy. 'Trump's Park Service Salary Donation Goes to Civil War Battlefield.' *The Hill*, 5 July 2017, thehill.com/policy/energy-environment/340704-trumps-park-service-salary-donation-goes-to-civil-war-battlefield.
3 Kruzel, John. 'Updated - Trump-O-Meter: Take No Salary.' PolitiFact, 26 July 2017, www.politifact.com/truth-o-meter/promises/trumpometer/promise/1341/take-no-salary/.

# 51. TRUMP TOOK THE ICE BUCKET CHALLENGE

Trump took the Ice Bucket Challenge—a fundraiser for the ALS Institute—in 2014. Miss USA and Miss Universe, whose beauty pageants he owned at the time, did the honors atop Trump Tower in Manhattan.

At the time, Trump said 'everybody' was challenging him and named three people (two if you consider one is an animated fictional character):

Homer Simpson, the 'star' of *The Simpsons*
Mike Tyson, retired heavyweight-boxing champion remembered for being a terrifying champion, a jailbird, and biting off pieces of Evander Holyfield's ears in 1997
Vince McMahon, the majority owner, CEO, and chairman of the WWE wrestling empire, and Trump buddy whose wife Linda Trump heads the US Small Business Administration

'I guess they want to see whether or not it's my real hair.' And…Trump's hair remained on his head. Nor did he flinch, and those buckets *were* full of ice. You can see the video here: http://www.eonline.com/news/574399/donald-trump-completes-the-als-ice-bucket-challenge-with-the-help-of-miss-universe-and-miss-usa-watch-now

Afterward, Trump challenged President Obama and his two older sons Don Jr and Eric. 'Let's go ladies,' he said.

Actually, Ethel Kennedy, widow of Sen. Robert Kennedy and the oldest living member of the Kennedy clan had already challenged President Obama. The challenge is to either submit to an ice dump or make a donation to the ALS Institute. Obama opted for the donation. (Hey, the guy's from Hawaii.)

Both Trump sons accepted their father's challenge. Don Jr, whose family dumped the ice on him, let out an impressive shriek. Eric stood stoically under a balcony as his fiancée (now wife) soaked him. He subsequently challenged his sister Ivanka and mother Ivana.

## 52. TRUMP SENT THE OWNER OF THE NEW YORK JETS TO BE AMBASSADOR TO BRITAIN

How is this a good thing? Ask any fan of the National Football League's (American football) New York Jets if they miss Woody Johnson.

Robert Wood Johnson IV is the great-grandson of Robert Wood Johnson I, who co-founded Johnson & Johnson, a $72-billion multinational manufacturer of pharmaceuticals, medical devices, and personal care products like baby powder now suspected of causing cervical cancer. But J&J is a household name in the US; it would be difficult to find a home without at least a couple of its products.

Woody bought the mediocre football team New York Jets in 2001 for $635 million. Not much has happened since to make the Jets any less of a disappointment to their long-suffering fans. They have made it to a wild card playoff game just six times since 2001 and twice to conference championship games; the last time was in 2010. You could say they have a lot in common with West Brom. [Dangerous and overconfident analogy for an American to make, delete. Ed. Come on you Baggies!]

Trump and Woody are old acquaintances through the shared bonds of football team ownership and being billionaires in the New York/New Jersey area. This no doubt influenced Trump's decision to give Woody the crown jewel of Presidential appointments: Ambassador to the United Kingdom. Oh, and Woody has been active in Republican politics for decades.

But why appoint a hapless (if still obscenely wealthy) trust-fund businessman to this plum position? *Because he's a fellow billionaire who won't ask for money*. The State Department never receives enough money in its budget to maintain ambassadorial holdings and let's face it, the US Embassy can't be seen serving cheese footballs, Tunnock's, and cartons of Ribena at receptions. *Bloomberg* says Johnson is worth $4.2 billion,[1] which should be enough to make

---

1 Coffey, Brendan. 'Jets Owner Woody Johnson Is Worth $4.2 Billion.' *Bloomberg*, 11 July 2017, www.bloomberg.com/news/articles/2017-07-11/ jets-owner-tapped-by-trump-as-u-k-ambassador-joins-500-richest.

sure the mansion is well stocked with the best offerings from Waitrose and Harrods. Pass the port!

Another plus is that Woody, who's a mellow kind of guy, has few eccentricities and won't do anything outrageous like sign a solid quarterback. He's been known to travel around New York City on a scooter and he once did a cross-country motorcycle trip with the actor Michael Douglas and *Rolling Stone* magazine founder Jann Wenner. He wore a helmet with fake black hair flying out behind him.

Certainly the Jets' head coach, Todd Bowles, breathed a sigh of relief when word of Woody's new job came out. Rumors had swirled about his potential sacking.

Looking at the Jets, though, one has to wonder if Woody is the man for the ambassadorial job, which for Trump means negotiating trade deals favorable to the US and the extra-tough job of persuading the British public that a visit from Donald Trump in 2018 is a good idea. As he said during his first speech as Ambassador, 'Many of you do not know the President. I have known him for over 30 years. Our sons were born three days apart in the same hospital…I can promise you, when you get to know him, you'll like him.'[2]

---

2 Alexander, Harriet. 'New US Ambassador to UK Woody Johnson Defends Donald Trump: 'When You Get to Know Him, You'll like Him'.' *The Telegraph*, 12 Sept. 2017, www.telegraph.co.uk/news/2017/09/12/new-us-ambassador-uk-insists-america-will-stand-britain-despite/.

## 53. TRUMP RESTORED CENTRAL PARK'S LANGUISHING WOLLMAN RINK

Wollman Rink is a public skating rink in New York City's Central Park. It opened in 1949 and was built through a donation from a woman named Kate Wollman in honor of her family, who founded a stock exchange firm in Kansas City. They later moved to New York (really, who wouldn't?) to open a second firm.

The rink was a popular ice-skating venue and hosted concerts in the summer. Led Zeppelin, Billie Holiday, and Pete Seeger are among the acts that played there to 5,000 seated fans and thousands more outside in Central Park.

By 1980, the rink was in terrible shape and had to be closed. Mayor Ed Koch hoped to have it restored within five years. But, as *The New York Post* says and this author's recollections agree, mismanagement and corrupt contractors prevented this from happening. The city wasted $13 million over five years.

Then, in June 1986, a handsome, rich—very, very rich—and fearless developer told the local media he could fix Wollman Rink in time for a Christmas opening. Impossible, the city said, but having 'nothing to lose,' told him to go for it. Koch, the *Post* says, 'held his nose and gave Trump the keys.'

Our hero, who had a bird's-eye view of the rink from his office, had a long-running feud with Mayor Koch over property taxes and other stuff that annoyed developers who have moved on from middle-class projects. By declaring a Wollman Rink Challenge, Trump had the opportunity to prove that private business can get things done better and faster than government. In this case, he was right.[1]

Trump wanted to pay for the Wollman Rink restoration himself but the city resisted. In the end, the two sides came to a deal in which the city would pay $3 million to cover restoration costs and Trump won the rights to operate the rink and open an adjacent restaurant, a sweet deal that continues to this day. Trump came out

---

1 Cuozzo, Steve. 'Saving Wollman Rink Made Trump a New York City Hero.' *New York Post*, 22 Jan. 2017, nypost.com/2017/01/22/saving-wollman-rink-made-trump-a-new-york-city-hero/.

*under budget* by $775,000—nearly one quarter—and opened the rink on November 1, eight weeks ahead of schedule.

The opening ceremonies featured Trump cutting a ribbon and performances by US skating stars and Olympic gold medalists Dorothy Hamill, Scott Hamilton and Dick Button. Button said the ice was so smooth he felt like he was 'skating on silk.'

It's hard to overstate how excited people were about the Wollman Rink's re-opening. Skating there remains a very popular past time for New Yorkers and tourists. With the Manhattan skyline in the near background, it really feels like you're in a film (and in fact, the rink has been featured in at least three). You can even rent the rink for private skating for two—'second to none when it comes to 'popping the question,' according to the rink's website at http://www.wollmanskatingrink.com/Default.aspx?p=DynamicModule&pageid=360149&ssid=268650&vnf=1

Sadly, there are no more summer concerts at the rink. It now hosts the Victorian Gardens Amusement Park each year.

## 54. TRUMP SYMPATHIZED WITH A YOUNG AIDS PATIENT AT A TIME WHEN MANY SHUNNED THOSE WITH HIV

Ryan White was a kid from Indiana. He was a hemophiliac and became infected with HIV after receiving a blood factor transfusion sometime in the early 1980s. He was diagnosed with AIDS in 1984 at age 12 and was told he would live for perhaps six months.

Although White's doctors stressed that he was not a public health threat because he was perfectly capable of keeping his body fluids to himself, local people rallied to kick him out of his school. Some were convinced he was an evil gay man out to infect the Heartland rather than a middle school student who read *GI Joe* comic books. I remember one news article described a piece of hate mail that called him a 'homophiliac.' His family's home and car were vandalized.

It was liberal Hollywood who embraced White, starting with Michael Jackson and Elizabeth Taylor. Elton John became a close friend who was with Ryan and his family when he died, and later performed at his funeral and served as a pallbearer.

Donald Trump naturally joined in—there were celebrities!—and contacted Ryan at least once during his frequent hospitalizations to wish him well. He has long claimed he offered Ryan use of one of his jets. White's mother, however, says the offer was never made. (Nor did Trump pay for Ryan's treatment, another rumor he did nothing to deny.)[1]

Trump did call on the family shortly after Ryan died in 1990. He was working with Jackson on a business deal when the call came that Ryan had died. He and Jackson flew together to Indiana.

After White's death, Congress passed and President George H W Bush signed legislation known as the Ryan White HIV/AIDS Act that provides health care services to people with HIV or AIDS. It pays

---

1 Gilmer, Maureen C. 'Is Trump a Bully? Ryan White's Mom Thinks So.' *Indianapolis Star*, 25 Oct. 2016, www.indystar.com/story/life/2016/10/24/trump-bully-ryan-whites-mom-thinks-so/92682232/.

for about 12 percent of AIDS services in the US. Trump's proposed budget does not target this particular program.

Trump's tenuous association with Ryan White hasn't translated into support for AIDS-related charities, of which there are many in New York. Perhaps the most disturbing incident came in 1996, when he appeared, uninvited, to a ribbon-cutting ceremony to open a school for young children with AIDS.

According to Abigail Disney, a respected documentarian and philanthropist (and great-niece of Walt Disney), Trump simply showed up and strolled to the podium. That's where then-Mayor Rudy Giuliani, former Mayor David Dinkins, a couple of chat show personalities, and major donors to the school were about to be seated. Trump took the chair intended for the donor who contributed the most money to the project.

Then he left without an explanation. 'What's wrong with you, man?' Disney recalled she thought to herself as she related the incident to *The Washington Post* in 2016.[2]

2 Fahrenthold, David A. 'Trump Boasts about His Philanthropy. But His Giving Falls Short of His Words.' *The Washington Post*, 29 Oct. 2016, www.washingtonpost.com/politics/trump-boasts-of-his-philanthropy-but-his-giving-falls-short-of-his-words/2016/10/29/.

## 55. MAR-A-LAGO WAS THE FIRST CLUB IN PALM BEACH TO WELCOME BLACKS, JEWS, AND GAY PEOPLE

Trump's Winter White House, Mar-a-Lago in Palm Beach, Florida, left the snooty society bunch there smoldering when he bought it in 1985 and declared membership would be open to anyone who could afford the fees. For 2017, this would reportedly be $200,000 for initiation, a $14,000 membership fee, plus $2000 for food. Money aside, there would be no social vetting process.

This is one place where 'they' really did throw the first stone. Trump offered the foundation that owned the property $25 million, a generous offer since it much of it had deteriorated after years of neglect. But the daughters of the property's original owner, Marjorie Merriweather Post, controlled the foundation. They refused the offer.

So Trump bought the beachfront lot in front of Mar-a-Lago for $2 million. Then he threatened to put up a wall to block its oceanfront view. 'My first wall,' he told *The Washington Post* in 2015. 'That drove everybody nuts. They couldn't sell the big house because I owned the beach, so the price kept going down and down.'[1]

In the end, he got Mar-a-Lago for just $7 million.

Once he took ownership of the property, the town of Palm Beach began to issue a list of restrictions. The club's membership had to be limited, as well as the number of people attending parties. Even photographers (the club planned to host beauty pageants) had to be limited so as to not 'offend' the billionaires next door.

Trump's lawyer sent the town council copies of the landmark films *Guess Who's Coming to Dinner* and *A Gentleman's Agreement* to underscore the history of racism and anti-Semitism at other clubs (Jews started their own clubs) and within the town. His inclusive club, however, was being singled out. A town council meeting that

1 Jordan, Mary, and Rosalind S. Helderman. Inside Trump's Palm Beach Castle. 14 Nov. 2015, www.washingtonpost.com/politics/inside-trumps-palm-beach-castle-and-his-30-year-fight-to-win-over-the-locals/2015/11/14/.

would normally last an hour or two went into the wee small hours and dropped some of the restrictions.

Once the club opened, Trump got acts like Billy Joel, Celine Dion, and Diana Ross to perform at Mar-a-Lago, no doubt to delighted guests. Michael Jackson and Lisa Marie Presley honeymooned there in 1994. Two other guests, actress J-Lo (Jennifer Lopez) and rapper/producer P. Diddy (Sean Combs) took a romantic walk on the beach on Easter Sunday 1998 and were later spotted having, um, intimate relations on a beach chair at the ultra-conservative Bath and Tennis Club down the way.

Like most private clubs, Mar-a-Lago doesn't make its membership list public but some names have been leaked. They are mostly extremely wealthy people from business, real estate, and conservative media. They also include people whose ethnic backgrounds wouldn't get them in most other Palm Beach clubs, such as Washington insider/lobbyist Ken Duberstein, Man United and Tampa Bay Buccaneers owner Avram Glazer, and even a local Democrat, real estate tycoon Jeff Greene.

## 56. TRUMP'S DEVELOPMENTS REVIVED DYING SECTIONS OF MANHATTAN

It's curiously overlooked that a lot of Trump developments revitalized areas of Manhattan that were dying or left for dead.

Let's start with Columbus Circle, where the Trump International Hotel and Tower is located. Before it was developed in the mid-1990s, Columbus Circle was dicey at best.

I first heard of the drug crack when a polite young dealer offered to sell me some as I walked through Columbus Circle one day in the mid-1980s. A few years earlier, I had persuaded some nervous friends to join me at a college fair at the fading New York Coliseum, now the site of the Time Warner Company headquarters. As the *New York Post* observes, Trump's hotel was the first project to 'reclaim Columbus Circle from the vagrants.' Today, it's a lovely place to stroll around and bustles with legal commerce, including a lot of OB-GYN surgeries.[1]

Perhaps no area has been transformed as completely as Grand Central Station. While it's always been a major commuting hub, it wasn't a place to hang around for very long in the 1970s and 80s. Drugs, drunks, and desperadoes ruled the area, and commuters hurried to get away from it as quickly as possible.

The Commodore Hotel symbolized the area's deterioration. It was built in 1919 to serve wealthy train travelers in its 2,000 rooms, had 'the world's largest lobby,' and ballrooms large enough to host a circus complete with elephants.

But as long distance train travel declined, so did the hotel. By 1977, it was sharing its ground floor with an 'X- rated massage parlor,' according to the *Post*. It was about to be shuttered when the Trump Organization purchased it in partnership with Hyatt Corporation. The partners spent $100 million to renovate the old hotel, which reopened as The Grand Hyatt in 1980.[1]

While this is one of the few Trump hotel deals that don't feature his name, the Trump Organization did oversee the rebuilding,

---

1 Cuozzo, Steve. 'How Donald Trump Helped Save New York City.' New York Post, 16 Nov. 2016, nypost.com/2016/02/07/how-donald-trump-helped-save-new-york-city/.

which retained some of the layout. Sadly, its Art Deco features were surrendered to jackhammers, according to the website Beyond the Gilded Age, where commenters speak of lost stone carvings, frescoes, and murals.[2]

Still, the hotel was a welcome change to the neighborhood and set the stage for Grand Central's renovation and restoration in the 1990s. Today, it's a destination not only to get home to Connecticut or wherever, but to eat at genuinely good cafes, shop, and hang out even if you aren't waiting for a train to (New) Jersey.

Why isn't this award-winning glass, steel, and masonry marvel a Trump-branded hotel? Because the partners fought a lot. Trump filed a civil racketeering lawsuit against Hyatt's owner, Jay Pritzker. Pritzker countered with a lawsuit saying Trump violated his partnership by failing to remain solvent (this was during his 1990s Atlantic City casino blowouts) and was improperly using the hotel for collateral to pay bank loans...you get the picture. In 1996, Pritzker bought out Trump for $140 million.[3]

2 'Beyond the Gilded Age.' The Commodore Hotel, 3 Nov. 2011, www. beyondthegildedage.com/2011/11/commodore-hotel.html.

3 Bagli, Charles V. 'Trump Sells Hyatt Share To Pritzkers.' *The New York Times*, 7 Oct. 1996, www.nytimes.com/1996/10/08/business/trump-sells-hyatt-share-to-pritzkers.html.

## 57. TRUMP ONCE PROFESSED A STARTLINGLY PROGRESSIVE AGENDA

Back in 2000, Trump was seriously considering running for President. He had joined the Reform party the previous year, and published his book *The America We Deserve*. In September of that year, he sat down to speak with *The Advocate*, a national news magazine that focuses on issues affecting LGBT people and communities.[1]

Reading this interview, it's hard to not feel a sense of longing for what could have been. You see a thoughtful person who isn't interested in dividing people—he just wanted 'the best and brightest' to come to Washington with him. There, they would work on universal healthcare, campaign finance reform (something he's barely uttered in recent years) and tax relief, which meant a one-time 14.25% tax on the 'superwealthy.'

Here's what could have been:

Condemnation of a racist politician. 'I used to like Pat [Buchanan].... then I read the things he had written about Hitler, Jews, blacks, gays, and Mexicans...it's disgusting. That speech he made at the '92 Republican convention was a disaster. He wants to divide Americans. Clearly, he has a love affair with Adolf Hitler, and that's sick. Buchanan actually said gay people had chosen 'satan and suicide.'

Asking the wealthiest to pay more, not less, in taxes. 'My plan to impose a one-time net worth tax of 14.25% on the superwealthy, when combined with our current projected surpluses [i.e., the Clinton surplus], will raise enough to pay off the national debt.'

Giving the middle-class a real tax break. The 'superwealthy tax' would save $200 billion in interest, Trump said. He would use half

1 'Donald Trump's Advocate Interview Where He Defends Gays, Mexicans.' *Advocate*, 28 Sept. 2015, www.advocate.com/election/2015/9/28/read-donald-trumps-advocate-interview-where-he-defends-gays-mexicans.

to cut taxes for the middle class and the other half to fund Social Security and to 'finance a new health care system.'

Universal health care. 'It's ridiculous that the richest country on Earth can't provide first-rate health care for our people. I would put forward a comprehensive health care program and fund it *with an increase in corporate taxes*...I like the Canadian system, although their health care is not the best.' (Italics are mine.)

Criticized the Christian Right for interfering with hate crimes legislation. Asked if he would support this legislation, Trump replied, 'Absolutely,' adding that that George W Bush 'had the opportunity...to show national leadership by passing a hate-crimes [sic] bill but didn't—presumably from pressure from the Christian right.'

'We must have a more tolerant society.' Trump was disturbed by the 1998 murders of Matthew Shepard, a gay university student beaten to death in Wyoming, and James Byrd, a middle-aged black man killed by white supremacists in Texas.

Two items are familiar: the number one focus on 'making the economy boom' (Make America Boom Again?) and ending 'the rip-off of America by our allies.' Then as now, Trump was frustrated by the US' role in providing the bulk of defense, presumably for NATO and in Japan and South Korea, while being 'screw[ed] with their trade policies.' Trump would have made himself the US Trade Representative, certainly an unusual move—and which would require Senate approval!

Many of these policies were outlined in his 2000 book *The America We Deserve*, in which he also states his support for outlawing assault weapons.

## 58. TRUMP IS RICH, BUT PROBABLY NOT AS RICH AS HE CLAIMS

How rich is Donald Trump? It's hard to know since he refuses to release his income taxes, a practice all Presidential candidates have followed since 1968.

Trump has claimed his net worth to be as high as $10 billion and includes the value of his brand in these estimates. In 2015, he told Fox News' Sean Hannity his annual income is $400 million and that he would spend all his liquid assets for a Presidential run.[1]

*Forbes* estimates that Trump's net worth is $3.1 billion as of September 2017.

$1.6 billion comes from New York City real estate
$500 million is from real estate outside New York
Another $570 million comes from golf courses and golf clubs
Trump brands are valued at $200 million
Cash and personal assets are $290 million[2]

Earlier in the year, *Forbes* estimated Trump's wealth at $3.5 billion, tied with nineteen other billionaires as the 544th-richest person on the planet. He dropped 220 spots from 2016 and lost a cool billion dollars. *Forbes* says this is due to fluctuations in the Manhattan real estate market, but according to the website NY.Curbed.com, its value as measured by square foot is the highest ever. Put it this way: a flat purchased in 2007 for $860,000 would sell for $1.1 million in 2016—an increase of almost 28%.[3]

One reason Trump gave for sitting out earlier Presidential races was that he didn't feel his children were ready to run the Trump Organization. By the time he announced his candidacy in 2015,

---

1 'Trump Says He Would Spend All His Liquid Assets on 2016 Run If He's Doing Well.' *Fox News*, FOX News Network, 12 Aug. 2015, https://goo.gl/n3vMMH.

2 'The Definitive Net Worth Of Donald Trump.' *Forbes*, Forbes Magazine, www.forbes.com/donald-trump/#998a83428992.

3 Nonko, Emily. 'Manhattan Apartment Prices Have Risen 28 Percent in One Decade.' *Curbed NY*, Curbed NY, 2 Feb. 2017, ny.curbed.com/2017/2/2/14483418/manhattan-home-sales-market-reports.

they apparently were. But if New York real estate is going up, just what *have* those kids been up to with the business?

An investigation by Politico in 2016 says Trump overvalues his properties, particularly his golf courses, which bring in more than half the income he claims. He also doesn't pay attention to expenses, which may be the real reason he won't release his income taxes. (His official excuse is that they are 'being audited' but they can still be released.) As the Trump Organization is privately held, it is not required to release its financial statements for public review.

But as a candidate for public office, Trump had to file financial disclosures with the Federal Election Commission (FEC), which enforces campaign finance laws for federal (e.g., US government) elections. The report the Trump campaign filed in May 2016 showed debts over $300 million, including $50 million of new debt, and sales of assets and securities for $15 million. If he is flush with cash, why the new debt and sales to raise more cash? Plus, he listed his assets at $1.5 billion, which apparently is his gross revenue, Politico reports. Net income, as we all know, can be much lower.[4]

Trump's apparent overvaluation of his golf courses has attracted attention from appraisers and New York State. In his FEC disclosure, Trump listed the value for the Trump National Golf Club in New York's Westchester County at $50 million. But tax attorneys for the Trump Organization put its at $1.35 million in an attempt to reduce its tax liability (they later raised it to $9 million).[4] Of course, a value won't translate into a sale price, but in this case the gap is so wide a case could be made for tax evasion, or at least tax avoidance.

4 White, Ben, et al. 'Shady Accounting Underpins Trump's Wealth.' *POLITICO*, 31 May 2016, www.politico.com/story/2016/05/donald-trump-money-net-worth-223662.

# 59. UNTRAINED ILLEGAL WORKERS WORKED ON THE TRUMP TOWER SITE

In 1980, Trump faced a potential lawsuit from about 200 workers from Poland who were forced to work 12-hour shifts to demolish a building on the site of the future Trump Tower after completing their daytime construction jobs at other sites. This violated (and still would) New York City laws.

Trump discovered the workers at a nearby construction site. He offered their boss, William Kaszycki, $775,000 to create a company that would employ the workers to demolish the Bonwit Teller. He promised an additional $25,000 if the work was completed quickly.[1]

But Kaszycki's workers specialized in window cleaning and cleaning up job sites. Nevertheless he accepted the offer and sneaked his crews over to the Bonwit Teller Teller Building on the future Trump Tower site. From 6 am to 6 pm, they worked on legitimate cleaning jobs, and were moved to the Trump site from 6 pm to 6 am. Some actually worked 24-hour shifts. This went on during the cold winter months of January to March, 1980.

These workers were not properly trained for demolition work, which is dangerous to put it mildly. They didn't even have basic safety equipment like hard hats. One worker was injured by a piece of falling steel, resulting in permanent disfigurement.

Kaszycki started spending more time in Florida (common for New Yorkers who want to escape the cold) and pay became sporadic. The workers hired a lawyer, a Polish-American named John Szabo. Unable to contact Kaszycki, Szabo contacted the Trump Organization to tell them he was prepared to obtain a mechanic's lien on the property if the workers weren't paid their back wages. This would halt construction by transferring some of the ownership to the workers themselves.

Trump insisted he had paid Kaszycki, who was supposed to pay the workers. He met with the workers and told them if Kaszycki

1 Calabresi, Massimo. 'Donald Trump and Undocumented Workers at Trump Tower.' *Time*, 24 Aug. 2016, time.com/4465744/donald-trump-undocumented-workers/.

were to quit, he'd pay them himself. But since he *had* paid them himself in the early days of the so-called contract, he effectively was their employer according to federal (US) law.

Even after Trump authorized one of his vice-presidents to pay the workers in cash, pay continued to be inconsistent. By the middle of 1980, the workers were owed more than $100,000. Szabo served several liens on the Trump Organization.

Szabo received a phone call in August 1980 from a 'Mr Barron' who said he was part of Trump's legal team to warn him Trump was going to sue for wrongful filing of liens. Trump later admitted at the ensuing trial that he and a senior Trump executive 'occasionally' used the pseudonym Barron, the name he gave his youngest son years later.

Szabo sent 'Barron' a long letter laying out his case. Then he received a letter from a real Trump lawyer advising him that Trump was threatening to call the government to deport the workers. Within a few weeks, Trump and Kaszycki were *both* under investigation for employing undocumented workers.

Working with the US Department of Labor, Szabo shared a $254,524 judgment against Kaszycki—not Trump—for violating the workers' safety and to pay the wages due to them.

# 60. TRUMP WAS SUCCESSFULLY SUED FOR FAILING TO PAY UNION PENSIONS

Harry Diduck was a former boxer and member of the Housewreckers Local 95 union whose members were working on the Trump Tower site. He discovered that Trump employed workers who were in the country illegally and concluded he had done so to avoid paying at least $300,000 due to the union pension fund if he had hired legal, unionized workers.[1]

Even worse, the illegal workers were paid between $4 and $5 per hour—half the amount paid to unionized workers, and sometimes even less. It's worth noting that nonunion workers in New York are required under law to be paid the same amount as those in a union.

Diduck hired a couple of lawyers and sued the Trump Organization for $600,000 in 1983; subsequent re-filings brought the amount up to $1 million. The case went on for 15 years. At one point, Trump walked out of a pretrial deposition after two hours, complaining that he was being harassed. A court order forced him to submit to another deposition.[1]

Trump testified at the 1990 trial that he did not know the workers were illegal. A labor consultant he had conferred with testified that he told Trump the workers were in the country illegally. Trump countered that the consultant was a 'peripheral advisor.'[2]

The judge ruled in 1991 that the Trump Organization conspired to withhold $325,000 in benefit payments plus interest, making the amount ultimately owed about $4 million. The Trump Organization appealed, and the appeals court ordered a retrial.[3]

The case was finally settled in 1999 when another, related case went to trial to decide if Trump or William Kaszycki were the

---

1 Massimo Calabresi, 'Donald Trump and Undocumented Workers,' 2016.

2 Baquet, Dean. 'Trump Says He Didn't Know He Employed Illegal Aliens.' *The New York Times*, 12 July 1990, www.nytimes.com/1990/07/13/nyregion/trump-says-he-didn-t-know-he-employed-illegal-aliens.html.

3 Robbins, Tom. 'Deal Sealed In Trump Tower Suit.' *NY Daily News*, 8 Mar. 1999, www.nydailynews.com/archives/news/deal-sealed-trump-tower-suit-article-1.834028.

illegal workers' legal employer. By then, Trump must have realized that directing Kaszycki to create a firm specifically to pay these particular workers would probably result in a judgment that he created a sham firm. The court might then find this firm, which he funded, was his and created to cover up the workers' legal status, pay them illegally low wages, *and* avoid paying into the union pension. This would also open up charges over the unsafe work environment and the illegal workers' lack of training in demolition techniques. So he settled the first case, and the second one was dropped. The details of the settlement have been sealed.

What of the Polish workers? *Time* interviewed one in 2016, who had actually gone to Trump's office to demand his pay. Now at age 80, the worker—who had also suffered permanent damage to his hand when a steel beam fell on it—had become a US citizen. He planned to vote for Trump.

# 61. THE TRUMP HOTEL IN WASHINGTON, DC WAS BUILT BY UNDOCUMENTED CONSTRUCTION WORKERS

If you think irksome, years-long lawsuits over hiring undocumented workers would deter Donald Trump from hiring 'illegals,' as he calls other people's employees, you're wrong. Lawsuits are a regular occurrence in Trumpland.

The Trump International Hotel just five blocks east of the White House is Washington's latest glitzy new hotel. It opened in September 2016 on the site of the Old Post Office Pavilion, a building on the US National Register of Historic Places. The bells in its iconic bell tower are replicas of those in Westminster Abbey and are known as the Bells of Congress. They were a gift to the US from Sir David Wills, founder of the Ditchley Foundation. The site itself is owned by the US government's General Services Administration, which agreed to lease it for 60 years to DJT Holdings LLC in 2013.

Trump's famous denouncement of illegal immigrants crossing over the Mexican border into the US –'drug dealers,' 'rapists', and 'I assume some are good people' really angered construction workers on the hotel site who were interviewed by the *The Washington Post* in 2015, many of whom were from Latin America. Several entered the US illegally and have since become US citizens through marriage or through various immigration programs, but others acknowledged they still held illegal status.

Many told *The Post* that they were worried about their jobs, presumably because they were undocumented. Others were disgusted by Trump's words. 'It's ironic,' said one worker from Mexico married to a US citizen. 'We're all here working very hard to build a better life for our families.' A sheet metal worker who crossed the border in the 1980s to escape the civil war in El Salvador said a judge granted him asylum and later became a citizen. 'Most of the concern is that this escalates,' the man said.

In spite of holding citizenship, he worried that Trump 'might come around one day and pretty much tell us to get the heck out of here.'[1]

Of course, Trump denied this and Hillary Clinton's assertion that he used illegal laborers to build Trump Tower (see Fact #59). 'I didn't hire one illegal immigrant to build Trump International Hotel on Pennsylvania Avenue,' Trump said at a rally in North Carolina, saying he used the E-Verify system, which researches all job applicants' backgrounds to verify their legal status. 'We didn't have one illegal immigrant on the job...believe me, we could have hired plenty.'[2]

But as anyone who's ever worked on a construction site knows, there are always subcontractors who may have employees who haven't been checked on E-Verify. E-Verify is a voluntary program; employers are not required to use it except for Federal (US) government work. Subcontractors are notorious for hiring day workers; even freelance workers are not (at least in my own experience) asked to prove their legal status by clients.

1 Olivo, Antonio. 'At Trump Hotel Site, Immigrant Workers Wary.' *The Washington Post*, 6 July 2015, https://goo.gl/jzzmMQ.
2 Shabad, Rebecca. 'Donald Trump Denies Using Undocumented Workers to Build New D.C. Hotel.' *CBS News*, 27 Oct. 2016, www.cbsnews.com/news/donald-trump-denies-using-undocumented-workers-to-build-trump-international-hotel/.

## 62. TRUMP OWNED A MODELING AGENCY THAT EMPLOYED UNDOCUMENTED MODELS

Trump started Trump Model Management in 1999. It became one of his most prized businesses for obvious reasons: he likes, almost needs, to be surrounded by models à la Hugh Heffner.

But in August 2016, the investigative journal *Mother Jones* broke a story that Trump Model Management hired foreign models who came to the US on tourist visas, which do not authorize the holders for employment.[1] Former models described living and working conditions straight out of *Oliver Twist*. They were packed into hot, cramped New York flats and constantly worried about being caught by the police—not for picking pockets, but for living and working in the country illegally.

Modeling agencies are not known to be nice employers; they expect long hours on the job and often put up models in dormitory-like housing. Trump's agency was known as among the worst to work for; the one model who gave her name, Rachel Blais, told *Mother Jones* 'they are the most crooked agency I've ever worked for, and I've worked for quite a few.'

In addition, this is an industry that quite commonly hired models who did not have permission to live, yet alone work, in the US. It's been said that Trump's wife Melania, who briefly worked for the agency, may have worked a few gigs herself when she first came to the US before obtaining the proper documentation.

Working for the Trump agency in 2004, Blais described living in an environment she described as 'like a sweatshop.' She shared a flat with four other models, sharing space of two tiny bedrooms with bunk beds; an additional mattress lay in a common area. Lying in her bunk, next to a window at street level, a vagrant once urinated on her through the window. 'It [was] like modern-day slavery.'

---

1  West, James. 'Former Models for Donald Trump's Agency Say They Violated Immigration Rules and Worked Illegally.' *Mother Jones*, 23 June 2017, www.motherjones.com/politics/2016/08/donald-trump-model-management-illegal-immigration/.

DONALD TRUMP IN 100 FACTS

Trump Model Management charged her as much as $1,600 per month to live there. Larger studio-style apartments in the area were let for less money.

At 18, Blais was the oldest resident; the youngest was 14. She recalls coaching the younger girls about how to answer to immigration officials when re-entering the US on tourist visas (she herself entered the US illegally through Canada).

Another model, Jamaican-born Alexa Palmer, who unsuccessfully sued the Trump agency in 2014 for wage theft and fraud, told *Mother Jones* she 'felt like a slave.' She was forced to pay large amounts of fees to the agency, on top of the 20% commissions she paid for each job it booked for her. Documents show she began working in the US nine months before she received authorization to do so.

Trump Model Management relied heavily on the US H1B visa program, which was intended to attract foreign talent to fill high tech jobs. Not only did Trump campaign against this program— 'they're stealing American jobs' was one of his mantras—he has tightened restrictions on it since becoming President.

Perhaps this is because he no longer needs H1B employees. In April 2017, an email leaked to *Mother Jones* revealed that Trump Models was going to end its operations.

# 63. AT LEAST SIX TRUMP BUSINESSES HAVE DECLARED BANKRUPTCY

While Trump has never personally declared bankruptcy, he has declared bankruptcy for six of his trademark businesses:

Trump Taj Mahal, Atlantic City, NJ (1991)
Trump Castle/Trump Marina Atlantic City (1992)
Trump Plaza and Casino, Atlantic City (1992)
Plaza Hotel, New York, NY (1992)
Trump Hotels and Casinos Resorts (a holding company for the casinos, 2004)
Trump Entertainment Resorts (another holding company for the casinos and The Plaza, 2009)

According to *Mother Jones*, 400 casino employees lost their jobs because of Trump mismanagement. Collectively, they lost $2 million in retirement savings.

Trump didn't lose out, though. He continued to collect a $2 million salary after Trump Marina's bankruptcy and took in $44 million as chairman of Trump Hotels and Casinos Resorts. 'I don't think it's a failure,' *Mother Jones* quotes him as saying. 'It's a success.'[1]

*Rolling Stone* listed Trump's 13 biggest business failures that include a few I'd forgotten about, such as the Trump Shuttle, which in 1988 had bought a spin-off of the US carrier Eastern Air Lines called the Eastern Shuttle. Trump defaulted on the loans he took out to buy the Eastern Shuttle in 1990 and turned the airline over to creditors. It eventually became part of US Airways, which merged with American Airlines in 2015, creating the American Airways Shuttle.[2]

1 Caldwell, Patrick. 'How Trump's Casino Bankruptcies Screwed His Workers out of Millions in Retirement Savings.' *Mother Jones*, 23 June 2017, www.motherjones.com/politics/2016/10/donald-trump-atlantic-city-bankruptcy/#.

2 Stuart, Tessa. 'Donald Trump's 13 Biggest Business Failures.' *Rolling Stone*, 14 Mar. 2016, www.rollingstone.com/politics/news/donald-trumps-13-biggest-business-failures-20160314.

Here are a few other businesses that didn't quite heap glory on the Trump brand:

Trump: The Game was created by the board game enterprise Milton Bradley in 1989. I recall it was billed as a more involved version of Monopoly and was supposed to be more like the real thing (although it apparently didn't come with illegal construction workers or tax lawsuits). Trump: The Game sold less than half of the two million units produced. Trump the person said it was too complicated for most people.

Trumpnet was registered as a telecommunications service in 1990 and the trademark was abandoned in 1992.

Trump Mortgage was launched in 2006, just as the US plunged into the (worldwide) recession caused by a collapsing real estate market. It closed shop a year later.

*Trump Magazine* came out in 2007, or so I've read. It was supposed to glide on the wings of advertising for high-end lifestyles, yachts etc. But then the recession happened and many luxury brands wisely chose to lay low so the magazine folded in 2009.

Trump University is probably the most-loathed Trump manifestation after big-game hunter Donald Jr. It was created to be a real estate school, with Trump's videotaped pledge that he personally developed curricula and personally chose instructors. Of course, none of this was true. It wasn't accredited by any of the dozens of accreditation groups in the US, it didn't grant college credits, or degrees, or even hand out grades. New York State's attorney general opened an investigation, and there were two class action suits that represented scores of ticked-off students. Trump is reported to have settled the suits for $25 million shortly after the 2016 election.

## 64. TRUMP SOLD PERSONAL PROPERTY, AN AIRLINE, AND BUSINESS INTERESTS TO SETTLE BUSINESS BANKRUPTCIES

US corporate law encourages incorporating businesses so that should they fail or be sued, the owner(s) aren't left bereft of funds. That's part of the reason why Trump and others like him are never obliged to declare personal bankruptcy. Another reason is that—as everyone knows—it really does pay to be rich. Trump likes to say he knows when to declare bankruptcy for a business. It also helps to have a yacht and airline to sell off to raise funds for more favorable settlements. Trump leveraged his personal properties and business interests to settle his major bankruptcy filings in Atlantic City and in one instance, New York City.

He sold his prized yacht, *Trump Princess*, for about $20 million in 1990 to come up with funds he needed for a favorable bankruptcy settlement for the first major bankruptcy, Trump Taj Mahal.[1] (The buyer, Saudi Prince Al Waleed bin Talal, was arrested in October 2017, reportedly to consolidate power for Saudi Crown Prince Mohammed bin Salman. Trump, a supporter of the Crown Prince, and Al Waleed have exchanged hostile comments via Twitter.) He also gave up half his ownership stakes in Trump Taj Mahal. Trump purchased the yacht for $29 million in 1987 from the Sultan of Brunei, who flipped it to him after buying it from its original owner, the Saudi businessman and reputed arms dealer Adnan Khashoggi who was having his own financial problems at the time.

Trump had to stop construction on a second yacht, *Trump Princess II*. Her hull was left at a Dutch shipyard, Amels, which Trump bought in 1990. Amels was sold two months later as bankruptcy was apparently looming for the following year. The hull remained at Amels until 2001; her fate is unknown.

The following year, 1992, Trump gave up half his ownership in The New York Plaza to Citibank as that property faced

1 'Serial Yacht Owners: Trump Princess.' *Yacht Harbour*, 8 Nov. 2016, yachtharbour.com/news/serial-yacht-owners--trump-princess-1247.

bankruptcy alongside his other Atlantic City casinos (Trump Plaza Hotel and Casino and Trump Castle Casino Resort.) Trump turned over majority control of Trump Hotel & Casino Resorts, which included yet another failed Atlantic City casino and a riverboat in Indiana. He remained the largest shareholder.

In late 1991, Trump sold the Trump Shuttle—which had actually run out of cash and defaulted on its debt in 1990—through an arrangement made by Citibank as it sought to settle Trump's default on its loans for The New York Plaza. By that time, the airline had been providing some charter operations, including Nelson Mandela's 1990 tour of the US. In 1990, it won a government contract to fly US military personnel to various US Air Force bases.

One victim of Trump Shuttle's closure was its sister helicopter service, Trump Air, which flew regular scheduled routes between in and around New York City, East Hampton, and Atlantic City. Trump Air ceased operations in 1992.

Trump gave up his remaining stakes in Trump Entertainment Resorts after it filed bankruptcy in 2009. He also resigned from the board, officially ending Atlantic City's Trump Era.

# 65. THOSE BANKRUPTCIES MADE TRUMP EVEN RICHER

Trump's personal wealth increased after these bankruptcies, thanks to the trend that emerged at the time in which US employers began shortchanging employees. Pensions for all but the most senior-level executives disappeared, saving businesses a bundle. Instead, they would match (perhaps up to 50%) their employees' contributions to so-called Individual Retirement Accounts (IRAs) that were managed by Wall Street firms with little interest or incentive to maximize the thousands of tiny accounts that sprang up.

Wages stagnated and 'at-will' employment in which employees could be dismissed for any reason became close to the norm in many states. (Few employees who found themselves out of a job could afford an attorney to sue when a sack was illegal.) All this benefited employers like Trump at the employees' cost, both monetarily and with regards to their mental health.

Freed from running casinos, Trump turned to writing books, or more accurately, hiring ghost writers to transcribe bits of business advice and wisdom. He'd already been published, starting with the combination autobiography and business text *The Art of the Deal*, a #1 bestseller for 13 weeks in 1987 that remained on *The New York Times*' bestseller list for 48 weeks. Ironically, his next book, *Trump: Surviving At The Top*, was published in 1990, just before the bankruptcies.

By 1997, with most (but not all) of the bankruptcies behind him, Trump released *Trump: The Art of the Comeback*. And in 2000, he released his pubic policy manifesto *The America We Deserve*. He unleashed a torrent of books in the new millennium.

DONALD TRUMP IN 100 FACTS

124

# 66. SPORTSWISE, THE DONALD TENDS TO DROP THE BALL

Trump hasn't enjoyed 'yoog' successes with American football in spite of the fact that even the least-valued National Football League (NFL) team is worth well over $1 billion.

In 1988, the owners of the New England Patriots approached Trump about buying the team. He turned them down because he believed the Patriots would be a bad investment. The team was then sold to Victor Kiam, known for Remington shaving products, for $87 million. The deal did not include Sullivan Stadium, the rather decrepit Patriots home.

Paper magnate Robert Kraft of International Forest Products, an old billionaire pal of Trump's, paid a bankruptcy court $25 million to buy Sullivan Stadium, which he later renamed Foxboro Stadium. A covenant required the team to continue playing there until 2001. Kiam sold the team to a creditor, James Busch Orthwein, for $110 million in 1992. Kraft bought the Patriots two years later for $158 million plus an agreement to pay off another $14 million of debt—at the time, the highest price ever paid for a sports team. A few years later, Kraft began building a new stadium, Gillette Stadium.

The Patriots have sold out every single game they have played at Gillette Stadium.

Kraft also introduced the concept of combining sports and entertainment centers. In 2007, he opened Patriot Place, a $350 million, 1.3 million square foot complex next to the stadium. Patriot Place includes a hotel that isn't a Trump property, shops, restaurants, cinemas, live entertainment, arcades, bowling, even an adjacent half-mile nature trail and cranberry bog.

Total investment from Kraft: $550 million.
Value of the Patriots, including Gillette Stadium: $3.7 billion in 2017.[1]

---

1 'New England Patriots on the Forbes NFL Team Valuations List.' *Forbes*, Forbes Magazine, www.forbes.com/teams/new-england-patriots/.

Value of Patriot Place: *Maybe* God knows. Kraft's net worth was estimated to be $5.2 billion in 2017. Trump's is a measly $3.5 billion.

In 2014, Trump attempted to purchase the Buffalo Bills after the owner died, but was rebuffed by the other NFL owners, who have to approve new ownership for any other team. Number of Super Bowls won by the New England Patriots: 5, all since 2002. Number of Super Bowls won by the Buffalo Bills: 0.

The Patriots are the second-most valuable NFL team, while Buffalo has the lowest valuation according to *Forbes*, although $1.6 billion is a pretty big price tag.

Trump once owned a football team, the New Jersey Generals, of the short-lived United States Football League (USFL), an alternate league that lasted from 1983 to 1985. Trump signed several NFL players to the Generals. Later, he bought another USFL team, the Houston Gamblers, and combined its players with the Generals. After the USFL closed, Trump joined a $1.7 billion antitrust lawsuit against the NFL.

The USFL party actually won this suit. A jury awarded them $1 in damages, tripled because that's how antitrust lawsuits work in the US. So, The Donald and the other USFL principals shared $3 in damages. They appealed the decision and lost. The US Supreme Court upheld the original court's decision and damages. A check for $3.76 (with interest) was issued to the USFL party. I'm pretty sure the lawyers will take most of it if it's ever cashed.

# 67. TRUMP WAS INDUCTED INTO THE PRO WRESTLING HALL OF FAME

Trump was inducted into the Pro Wrestling Hall of Fame for WWE pro wrestling entertainment in 2013, a mere three years before being elected President. His involvement with WWE dates to the late 1980s, when the now-defunct Trump Plaza in Atlantic City, New Jersey, hosted WrestleMania.

In 2007, Trump got into the act on WWE's *Monday Night Raw* program when he addressed its chairman, Vince McMahon, on the Jumbotron screen during a Fan Appreciation Night. 'The best way I know to show my appreciation to the audience, even if it's your audience,' he declared, 'is to give them what everybody wants, me in particular: money! Money, Vince! Money, money, money.'

('Money money money' is also the chorus for the O-Jays song 'For the Love of Money,' *The Apprentice's* theme song.)

Tens of thousands ('buckets of cash!') of $10, $20, $50, and $100 bills showered down from the rafters to cheering fans below.

McMahon stormed around the arena in a highly dramatic fashion shouting that it was his own money Trump had dumped. He challenged Trump to a Battle of the Billionaires at the upcoming WrestleMania 23. The winner would get to shave the loser's head.

Like good billionaires, they hired stand-in wrestlers. Trump's was Bobby Lashley, at the time the reigning Extreme Championship Wrestling champ. McMahon's champion was Umaga, a veteran of both WWE and All Japan Pro Wrestling.

Before the match, Trump and McMahon faced off one another over a small boardroom-like table set in the ring, flanked by their champs, to sign a contract. McMahon wore pinstripes while Trump opted for a somber black suit livened up with a bright fuchsia tie.

A retired pro wrestler, Stone Cold Steve Austin, presided over the match, which Umaga/McMahon lost. Trump triumphantly shaved McMahon's head. Although Stone Cold Steve had helped strap McMahon down for the shaving, he ended the evening with a toned-down version of his trademark 'Stunner' to Trump—a kick to the chest that knocked Donald flat. Austin strolled out of the ring as Lashley anxiously knelt beside a prone Trump.

In 2009, Trump and McMahon put on a fake act to make it look like Trump purchased *Monday Night Raw*. He announced the deal via Jumbotron during a *Raw* taping and was immediately booed. That turned to cheers when he announced it would air commercial-free and that fans who paid for tickets would get a full refund.

This all looked very real, particularly when USA Network, which aired the show, put out a phony press release announcing McMahon was selling the *Raw* program to Trump. *Raw* is part of WWE, which is a publicly traded company, and the move caught its investors off guard. The stock immediately began to tank.

Trump's 'ownership' plans continued and McMahon, who couldn't stand seeing WWE's value continue to drop, 'bought' *Raw* back at twice the supposed purchase amount.

# 68. TRUMP ONCE PRODUCED A BROADWAY SHOW

Way back in 1970, a 23-year old named Donald Trump made one of his first deals fresh out of university: to put up 50% of the cost for *Paris is Out!*, a play its producer hoped to open on Broadway. Trump's offer was contingent on getting equal billing as a producer.

It wasn't real estate, but it was something and the play's champion, producer David Black, was impressed that the young guy who visited his office in the Broadway district had done his homework—he'd read the play and read up on him. His resumé at that point included producing 18 Broadway plays in the 1960s, picking up Tony awards on the way.[1]

The two agreed that Black would serve as lead producer and make all the decisions on *Paris is Out!*, a comedy that turned out to be more or less a flop. The theater critic Walter Kerr wrote 'I neither hated it nor liked it. I simply sat there and looked at it'[2] and another, Clive Barnes, wrote that he 'pitied it.'[1] It played for 112 performances and closed. Trump never produced another play.

In 1992, Trump's wife Marla Maples joined the cast of *The Will Rogers Follies*, a Broadway musical comedy in which she played the girlfriend of the showman Florenz Ziegfeld. Her appearance boosted sales as people wanted to see 'the woman who stole Ivana's husband.' A sure laugh every night came from the actress who played Ziegfeld's wife, who asked Maples' character 'How did you get this part?' To her credit, Maples would roll her eyes to milk more laughs.

In October, 2017, Trump re-emerged on Broadway via Twitter, where he engaged in a particularly nasty fight with filmmaker

---

1 Paulson, Michael. 'For a Young Donald J. Trump, Broadway Held Sway.' *The New York Times*, 6 Mar. 2016, www.nytimes.com/2016/03/07/theater/for-a-young-donald-j-trump-broadway-held-sway.html?

2 Staff, Inside Edition. 'Donald Trump Was Once a Broadway Producer On Short-Lived Show.' Inside Edition, 16 Mar. 2016, www.insideedition.com/headlines/15290-donald-trump-was-once-a-broadway-producer-on-short-lived-show.

and artist/activist Michael Moore, who had just ended a limited comedy on Broadway, *Terms of My Surrender*. The show, which included a call to revolt against Trump among other comedy skits such as 'Stump the Canadian,' did OK at the box office. But Trump tweeted out that 'the Sloppy Michael Moore Show on Broadway was a TOTAL BOMB and was forced to close. Sad!'

Moore tweeted back in 10 tweets. The last two noted that the show was a 12-week-only run 'due to my commitment to my upcoming primetime TV series and movie' and 'On Broadway, Donald, they call it a 'LIMITED ENGAGEMENT'—just like we're planning on making your presidency.'

In July 2017, Tony-winning playwright Tony Kushner (no relation to Trump's son-in-law Jared) revealed that he is writing a play about Trump that will be set two years prior to the election. The work would be a challenge, he told *The Daily Beast*, as Trump is 'the kind of person, as a writer, I tend to avoid as I think he is borderline psychotic.'[3]

Kushner is best known for his two-part series *Angels in America*, in which Trump's mentor Roy Cohn is the play's chief villain.

3 Teeman, Tim. 'Tony Kushner: Why I'm Writing a Play About Donald Trump.' *The Daily Beast*, 19 July 2017, www.thedailybeast.com/tony-kushner-why-im-writing-a-play-about-donald-trump.

# 69. BROTHER FREDDY'S STRUGGLE WITH ALCOHOL DIDN'T STOP TRUMP FROM STARTING A VODKA BRAND

Trump launched his own brand of vodka in 2005. He predicted that Trump Vodka mixed with tonic—the 'T&T'—would become the most popular cocktail in the U.S. Its slogan was 'Success Distilled.'

But Trump Vodka was, according to *Bloomberg News*, 'a flamboyant exercise in failure.'

J. Patrick Kenny, founder of Drinks America, approached Trump about using his name for a vodka brand just as *The Apprentice* was topping the ratings. He met with Trump in his office/stage and as cameras started rolling, Trump vowed to 'negotiate the shit out of you,' Kenny told *Bloomberg*. He agreed to lend his name to the vodka in exchange for half the profits, or a $2 million minimum—even though the company's shares were selling for less than a dollar each.[1]

It didn't help that the vodka's namesake didn't drink, which became a problem as Trump held numerous interviews with New York media discussing the evils of alcohol. 'I'm not a proponent of drinking,' he said in one interview. 'You see [drinkers] being carried out of an office, they're totally bombed, and you totally lose respect for them,' he said, adding that he would use some of the profits to fund addiction research.

Even the Netherlands-based distiller, who introduced himself 'as the best vodka producer' couldn't describe the flavor because he 'wasn't a vodka drinker.'

Drinks America folded in 2012. Trump sued distributors in Israel and Germany for using his name and image without permission. They later came to a licensing agreement. Later, Trump bought a vineyard in Virginia—'the largest winery on the East Coast.'

1  Abelson, Max. 'On the Rocks: The Story of Trump Vodka.' *Bloomberg*, 20 Apr. 2016, www.bloomberg.com/features/2016-trump-vodka/.

# 70. TRUMP SHOPS OUTSIDE THE USA TO MAKE HIS BRANDS AND BUY CONSTRUCTION MATERIALS

While Trump bitterly criticizes Apple and other companies that outsource their work, it turns out that many of his own brands are also outsourced.

The Donald J. Trump Signature Collection of menswear, which includes ties, dress shirts, suits, accessories like cufflinks, wallets, and glasses, is mostly produced in factories in China and Bangladesh. Trump has said that there are no American companies who manufacture these products, which is patently untrue. For example, Brooks Brothers ties are produced in New York City, and most of its suits are made in Massachusetts. North Carolina and Massachusetts are home to two popular materials—selvedge denim and GoreTex.

There's plenty of branded eyewear made in the US. Visionworks, a major eyeglass and eye care chain, has five labs that make glasses and sunglasses, all located in the US. One eyewear company, Shuron, has been around since 1865!

Not only does Trump accessorize outside the US, he buys from nations like China whose trade policies he criticizes. Sad!

Trump complained during a debate with Hillary Clinton that China 'dumps steel' in the US, but he apparently can't resist the bargain. China has been his favorite source for steel. The Trump International Hotel in Las Vegas and the Trump International Hotel and Tower in Chicago, where a bottle of Trump Ice Natural Spring Water from the minibar will set you back $25, were built in 2005 with Chinese steel.

Interestingly, the loans Trump obtained to finance the Chicago project came from hedge funds financed by George Soros, an immigrant billionaire demonized by Trump and right-wing conservatives for his backing of liberal candidates and projects.

In spite of his fierce criticism of the Trans-Pacific Partnership and pulling the US out of it, Trump apparently had no problem importing goods for his hotels through TPP. According to *Business*

*Insider*, rooms inside Trump-owned hotels include headboards, mirrors, and minibar technology from China; slippers, golf club head covers, and hangers from Hong Kong; and ice buckets and note pads and penholders from Thailand. [1]

Trump Home Furnishings, which includes a surprising number of alcohol-related goods like barstools and cocktail tables, are, according to its website, 'Handcrafted to Perfection and made to order.' Furthermore, they are 'engineered using elite and exotic materials attained from around the world.'

At least the $25 bottles of Trump Ice Natural Spring Water are sourced from springs in Vermont and New York, where it's also bottled.

Trump Fragrances, which include *Empire By Trump* and *Success By Trump* (the latter 'captures the spirit of the driven man') are manufactured in the US.

Trump does hold firm on personally boycotting some imports. When the baked products manufacturer Nabisco moved some of its jobs to Mexico, he vowed to never eat another Oreo cookie. Now *that's* patriotism.[2]

1 Varinsky, Dana. 'Trump's 'Buy American' Policy Directly Conflicts with How His Own Hotels Operate.' *Business Insider Australia*, 28 Jan. 2017, www.businessinsider.com.au/trump-hotel-imports-2017-1.
2 Helderman, Rosalind S., and Tom Hamburger. 'Trump Has Profited from Foreign Labor He Says Is Killing U.S. Jobs.' *The Washington Post*, WP Company, 13 Mar. 2016, goo.gl/cX2KZF

# 71. TRUMP OWNS 16 GOLF COURSES

Trump has been playing golf since at least his college days, and it's a good bet he took up the game as a teenager or even earlier. As much as he loves the game, he didn't buy his first golf property until 1999, when he purchased a 300-acre parcel next to the Palm Beach International Airport. This became the Trump International Golf Club.

Trump didn't exactly plan on building a golf course. He saw an advert for a 215-acre parcel Palm Beach County was trying to lease. At the time, he was suing the county over airport noise pollution—he was annoyed by planes flying directly over Mar-a-Lago—for $75 million. So he made the county an offer: he would drop the lawsuit in exchange for a 30-year lease. The county accepted and allowed him an unlimited budget to develop the land. Trump estimates he spent $40 million to transform it into an 18-hole course designed by Jim Fazio and an adjacent private club.

Between 1999 and 2017, Trump built or acquired another 15 courses around the world:

1. Trump Turnberry, Turnberry, Scotland
2. Trump International Golf Links, Aberdeen, Scotland
3. Trump International Golf Links, Doonberg, Ireland
4. Trump National Doral, Miami, Florida
5. Trump National Golf Club, Jupiter, Florida
6. Trump Golf Links, Ferry Point, New York
7. Trump National Golf Club Hudson Valley, Hopewell Junction, New York
8. Trump National Golf Club Westchester, Briarcliff Manor, New York
9. Trump National Golf Club, Los Angeles, California
10. Trump National Bedminster, Bedminster, New Jersey—also Trump's weekend getaway
11. Trump National Golf Club, Colts Neck, New Jersey
12. Trump National Golf Club Philadelphia, Pine Hill, New Jersey

13. Trump National Golf Club, Charlotte, North Carolina
  14. Trump National Golf Club Washington, DC, Potomac Falls, Virginia
  15. Trump World Golf Club, Dubai, UAE

Trump's golf courses are designed by top architects like Fazio, Greg Norman, Jack Nicklaus, and most recently, Tiger Woods, who designed the Dubai course. Many of these courses are highly ranked and have hosted championship professional tournaments.

Two more golf courses and clubs are under construction in Indonesia. One will be in Lido City, West Java, with a course designed by Ernie Els, and the other in Bali.

Many tournaments pulled out from Trump courses after his comments in his June 2015 candidacy announcement in which he said Mexican immigrants bring drugs and crime. 'They're bringing drugs. They're bringing crime. They're rapists. And some, I assume, are good people.[1]

First, the PGA cancelled its Grand Slam of Golf scheduled to be held at Trump's Los Angeles Club in October 2015 and removed the club from its circuit. In 2016, the PGA moved its World Golf Championships event from the Doral to the Club de Golf Chapultepec in Mexico City.

The PGA eventually recovered from its outrage. By May 2017, it was playing its Senior Championship tournament at the Virginia course just outside Washington, DC, and had already signed to play the 2022 PGA Championship in Bedminster.

1 'Here's Donald Trump's Presidential Announcement Speech.' Time, 16 June 2015, http://time.com/3923128/donald-trump-announcement-speech/.

## 72. TRUMP HAS PUBLISHED 12 BOOKS, MOSTLY ABOUT HIMSELF; AT LEAST ONE CO-AUTHOR DEEPLY REGRETS HIS ROLE

Aspiring authors are often told to write about what they know. In Trump's case, this means writing about himself under the guise of business advice, self-help, and public policy.

Trump's first book, *Trump: The Art of the Deal*, was published in 1987. It was co-written with Tony Schwartz, who spent much of 2016 agonizing over his role in 'putting lipstick on a pig,' as he told Jane Meyer of *The New Yorker* in an angst-filled interview. 'I feel a deep sense of remorse that I contributed to presenting Trump in a way that brought him wider attention and made him more appealing than he is.' Today, he says, he would call the book *The Sociopath*.[1]

Shortly before the article was published, Trump called Schwartz after speaking with a *New Yorker* fact-checker. 'I think you're very disloyal,' he told Schwartz. 'Have a nice life.' Then he hung up.[2]

*The Art of the Deal* was a 'yoog' seller, reaching the Number One spot on *The New York Times* Best Seller List where it remained for 13 weeks. It stayed on the list for another 48.

In 1990, he released *Trump: Surviving at the Top*, co-written with Charles Leerhsen. Ironically, this came out just as his bankruptcies in Atlantic City were starting to pile up.

Bankruptcy takes a lot of time away from work, even when you have a ghostwriter/co-author doing the heavy lifting, so the next Trump book, *Trump: The Art of the Comeback* didn't come out until 1997. Both of Trump's ex-wives denied the reasons he gave in the book for their divorces: Ivana talked about work too much, and Marla bugged him to come home from work.

---

1 Mayer, Jane. 'Donald Trump's Ghostwriter Tells All.' *The New Yorker*, 31 July 2017, www.newyorker.com/magazine/2016/07/25/donald-trumps-ghostwriter-tells-all.

2 Schwartz, Tony. 'I Wrote The Art of the Deal with Trump.' *The Washington Post*, 16 May 2017. https://goo.gl/Vdpuiz.

One person who really benefitted from the book was co-author Kate Bohner, who became the subject of a Candace Bushnell profile (who later wrote *Sex and the City*) about her life during this time.

The new millennium saw a downright slew of Trump books, all written with various co-authors. Here's a partial list:

*The America We Deserve* (2000)
*Trump: The Way to the Top* (2004)
*Trump: Think like a Billionaire* (2004)
*Trump: How to Get Rich* (2004)
*Trump: The Best Real Estate Advice I Ever Got: 100 Experts Share Their Strategies* (2006)
*Trump 101: The Way to Success* (2006)
*Trump: Think Big and Kick Ass in Business and Life* (2007)

*The America We Deserve* was co-authored with Dave Shiflett, who recounted his experiences in the *Boston Globe* among other places. 'I found Trump to be funny, truly concerned about America's future, and a guy who paid his bills on time.' (A lot of Atlantic City vendors would vigorously disagree: see Fact #78.) But Shiflett also predicted in a January 2016 article that if Trump were elected, 'The shock to the system would be profound and first noticeable by the words that tumble out of his mouth. It's not unreasonable to expect that he would become the first chief executive to use the F-word.'[3]

3 Clary, Timothy A. 'Donald Trump's America – The Boston Globe.' *BostonGlobe.com*, 17 Jan. 2016, www.bostonglobe.com/ideas/2016/01/17/ donald-trump-america/lAGa5CEKgZD6xJx2F5KNGM/story.html.

## 73. TRUMP HAS APPEARED IN AT LEAST 13 FILMS AND 19 TELEVISION SERIES

While Trump's TV career is best known for *The Apprentice* and *The Celebrity Apprentice*, he's also appeared as a guest star in at least 17 other shows:

*100 Greatest TV Quotes & Catchphrases*
*American Experience*
*The Drew Carey Show*
*The Fresh Prince of Bel-Air*
*Great Projects: The Building of America*
*Inside the Actors Studio*
*Intimate Portrait (Ivana Trump)*
*It's Good to Be...*
*The Job*
*The Nanny*
*Reality Stars Uncensored*
*Saturday Night Live*
*Sex in the City*
*Suddenly Susan*
*Treasures of New York*
*True Hollywood Story*
*When I Was 17*

*The Apprentice* ran from 2004 to 2008. It had its highest ratings during the first season. Subsequent seasons pitted male and female contestants and street smarts versus book smarts. In 2005, Trump discussed having black and white contestants compete against one another on *The Howard Stern Show*, a concept 'thrown out by some person.' Stern's co-host, Robin Quivers, suggested this could start a riot and when Stern followed up on this, Trump said he would handle it 'beautifully. Because as you know, I'm very diplomatic...I'm a sensitive person.'[1]

---

1 Smith, Candace. 'Donald Trump Considered Blacks vs Whites Version for 'The Apprentice'.' ABC News, 20 May 2016, abcnews.go.com/Politics/donald-trump-considered-blacks-whites-version-apprentice/story?id=39259585.

Trump has also appeared on several news magazine shows like *Extra*, which focuses on Hollywood, and popular investigative shows like *202/20, 60 Minutes, Dateline, Nightline,* and *CNBC Titans*. He has been a guest on chat shows including *The Oprah Winfrey Show*. And of course he's pretty regular on Fox News.

The only film I could recall seeing Trump appear in is *Home Alone 2: Lost in New York*. His other film credits include:

*54*
*An Inconvenient Truth: Truth to Power*
*The Associate*
*Celebrity*
*Eddie*
*Ghosts Can't Do It*
*Giuliani Time*
*Kings of Kallstadt*
*The Greatest Movie Ever Sold*
*The Little Rascals*
*Two Weeks Notice*
*Zoolander*

Trump has almost always appeared as himself, although he was cast as 'Waldo's Dad' in *The Little Rascals* and as a VIP patron in *54*. He received a star on the Hollywood Walk of Fame in 2007. The star isn't exactly recognition of his star power, but rather, recognition of his role as producer of the Miss Universe pageants, which were televised. Stars are purchased from the Hollywood Chamber of Commerce.

In October 2016, a man dressed as a construction worker took a pickaxe and sledgehammer to Trump's star. Police say he wanted to remove the star and auction it to raise money on behalf of women who have accused Trump of sexual assault. But those stars are pretty well embedded, so he quit after five minutes of inflicting minor damage. The star has since been replaced.

This isn't the first time Trump's star has been targeted. It had already been painted over and sprayed with graffiti and in July 2016, someone erected a tiny barbed-wire fence with American flags around it.

# 74. THERE ARE MANY, MANY LAWSUITS FROM THE SUIT

While the Trump Organization, its offshoots and predecessors, and Trump himself have been the focus of a lot of lawsuits, Trump is no slouch when it comes to filing suits himself. Aaron Elstein, a senior reporter for *Crain's New York Business*, estimated in 2015 that Trump had been personally involved in New York courts 65 times, while Trump Tower was in lawsuits 45 times and Trump Plaza (New York) a whopping 109 times.[1]

Some suits are understandable. You just can't let someone like Bill Maher get away with saying your mother mated with an orangutan. Trump sued the comedian over this comment for $5 million in 2013 but dropped the case after a few weeks.[2]

Trump sued Palm Beach County over airport noise, claiming air traffic was being sent over Mar-a-Lago. He later dropped the suit in exchange for a favorable deal to purchase land that became one of his golf courses.

Trump sued other Trumps, too, as Elstein discovered. In 1984, he sued developers Jules and Eddie Trump for trying to muscle into New York real estate with 'his' name. The brothers, who emigrated from South Africa with their Lithuanian Jewish parents, developed properties in Florida and came to Donald's attention when they purchased a pharmacy chain that had stores in New York. (An industry trade magazine mistakenly sent Donald a congratulatory letter.) Trump lost his suit. He then petitioned the US Patent and Trademark Office to revoke the brothers' registration of the name The Trump Group. This time he sort of won: the parvenu Trumps can still use the name The Trump Group but they can't register it.[1]

Trump's first wife Ivana was also a lawsuit target. He sued her shortly after their 1992 divorce for $25 million, claiming she broke

DONALD TRUMP IN 100 FACTS

1 Elstein, Aaron, and Bloomberg. 'The Notorious Case of The Donald vs. Trump.' *Crain's New York Business*, 6 Aug. 2015, www.crainsnewyork.com/article/20150806/BLOGS02/150809914/the-notorious-case-of-the-donald-vs-trump.

2 Nuzzi, Olivia. 'Donald Trump Sued Everyone but His Hairdresser.' *The Daily Beast*, The Daily Beast Company, 6 July 2015, www.thedailybeast.com/donald-trump-sued-everyone-but-his-hairdresser

their agreement and disclosed details about his finances.[2] It's not known how this was settled but they appear to have a calmer relationship today than in the days following their separation, when Ivana signed papers accusing him of rape, an allegation she later withdrew.

In 1993, Trump filed an unsuccessful lawsuit against the US Government for giving Native Americans exclusive rights to operate casinos on tribal land. Later that year, he loudly accused tribes of permitting organized crime to run 'rampant' on reservations, shouting 'people know it, people are talking about it. It's going to blow!' during a Congressional hearing.[3]

In 2006, he greeted the New Year by filing a lawsuit against Timothy O'Brien, an author and highly respected journalist whose first book, *Trump Nation*, reported that people close to Trump estimated his wealth at no more than $250 million. Trump sued him for $5 billion, claiming this damaged his reputation. The suit was dismissed in 2009 and a 2011 appeal was rejected.[4]

In 2012, Trump sued someone you would assume would be a personal favorite of his: a beauty pageant contestant. Miss USA 'loser' Sheena Monnin had written in a Facebook post that the pageant was 'rigged' because the five finalists were selected before it even began. A court ordered her to pay $5 million in damages.[2]

3  Michael D'Antonio, *Never Enough*, 2015.
4  Tuttle, Ian. 'The Litigious – and Bullying – Mr. Trump.' *National Review*, 19 Feb. 2016, www.nationalreview.com/article/431575/donald-trump-tim-obrien-courtroom-story.

# 75. AT LEAST 24 WOMEN HAVE ACCUSED TRUMP OF INAPPROPRIATE BEHAVIOR

Trump infamously bragged to Billy Bush, formerly of *Access Hollywood*, that he grabs women by their private parts because '[he] can do anything.' He also said that when he wants to kiss a beautiful woman, 'I just start kissing them. It's like a magnet...I don't even wait. And when you're a star, they let you do it. You can do anything.'[1]

So it isn't particularly surprising that alleged abuse dates to the 1980s, when sexual harassment was in fact common and not considered particularly outrageous—other than to the targets of such behavior. Trump has denied the accusations, singly and together, on Twitter, in Presidential debates, and through his campaign press spokeswoman and later, the White House Press Secretary.

After watching the second Presidential debate, in which Trump denied he had actually done the things he bragged about to Bush, several women became angry enough to come forward with their stories.

Businesswoman Jessica Leeds says Trump groped her on a flight as they sat next to one another in a first-class cabin in the 1980s. 'He was like an octopus...his hands were everywhere.' She fled to the back of the aircraft.[1] Leeds' story was confirmed by four other people she confided in shortly after the incident.

Rachel Crooks was a 22-year old receptionist for a real estate investment and development company in Trump Tower in 2005. She says she encountered Trump outside an elevator and introduced herself. They shook hands and Trump proceeded to kiss her on the cheeks and then on the mouth. 'It was so inappropriate...he thought I was so insignificant that he could do that.' After getting away from Trump, she immediately called her sister in Ohio, who confirmed she related the incident.[2]

---

1 *Transcript: Donald Trump's Tape Comments About Women.* 8 Oct. 2016, www.nytimes.com/2016/10/08/us/donald-trump-tape-transcript.html.

2 Barbaro, Megan Twohey And Michael. 'Two Women Say Donald Trump Touched Them Inappropriately.' *The New York Times*, 12 Oct. 2016, www.nytimes.com/2016/10/13/us/politics/donald-trump-women.html?_r=0.

Most of the allegations take place in the 1990s, a time when Trump was busy producing beauty pageants, clubbing, and rumored to be dating several models.

Temple Taggart competed in the Miss USA pageant the first year it was under Trump's ownership. She told *The New York Times* that Trump's forward manner with her and other contestants was startling. 'He kissed me directly on the lips. I thought, 'Oh, my God, how gross.' I think there were a few other girls that he kissed on the mouth. I thought "wow, that's inappropriate."'[3]

Trump breezed through the changing room at Miss Teen USA 1997, where contestants as young as 15 were in various states of undress. 'Don't worry, ladies, I've seen it all,' Mariah Billado, the former Miss Vermont Teen USA, recalls him telling them. Three contestants told *Buzzfeed* they recall seeing him in the dressing room. Two said it was 'shocking' and 'creepy.'[4] Trump bragged on *The Howard Stern Show* that he was 'allowed to go in' the dressing rooms 'because I'm the owner of the pageant… You know, they're standing there with no clothes…these incredible looking women, and so I sort of get away with it.' Billado says she told Ivanka, who co-hosted the pageant, about her father in the dressing room. 'Yeah, he does that,' she answered.[4]

3 Barbaro, Michael, and Megan Twohey. 'Crossing the Line: How Donald Trump Behaved with Women in Private.' *The New York Times*, 14 May 2016, www.nytimes.com/2016/05/15/us/politics/donald-trump-women.html.

4 Taggart, Kendall, et al. 'Teen Beauty Queens Say Trump Walked In On Them Changing.' *Buzzfeed*, 13 Oct. 2016, www.buzzfeed.com/kendalltaggart/teen-beauty-queens-say-trump-walked-in-on-them-changing/.

# 76. TRUMP STEAKS TANKED WHILE REVIEWS OF TRUMP STEAKHOUSES ARE MIXED

If you never heard of Trump Steaks, it's ok: the business only lasted for two months in 2007.

Trump Steaks was created for The Sharper Image, a gadget store men in the US really, really liked. Although the brick-and-mortar stores dried up, it lives on as an e-commerce site and continues to sell mostly silly and expensive items.

Trump Steaks, though, hardly sold at all. They were only sold through the store's catalog, but heavily marketed in the stores, where people could order $200 worth of filet mignon, rib eyes, and burgers. Somehow, it just didn't happen.

Reviews were mixed. According to the admittedly liberal Think Progress website, they ranged from 'worst burger EVER!' and 'extremely greasy' to 'tender, juicy, and absolutely among the best-tasting steaks I've cooked on my home grill,' from one food editor. *Gourmet*, though, called them 'edible but not particularly good.'[1]

Trump, of course, promised that his steaks were 'The World's Greatest Steaks.' You can see his video here: https://www.youtube.com/watch?time_continue=24&v=LyONt_ZH_aw

Trump does love a good, well-done steak, which he eats with ketchup. He frequently eats at steakhouses, and steak restaurants are prominent in his hotels. Like his steaks, they have mixed reviews.

The latest one to open, BLT Prime at the Trump International Hotel in Washington, DC got a good review from the *Washington Post,* whose critic praised its 'terrific service' lack of 'bad tables' and great burgers made with dry-aged beef. Moreover, *The Post* says the seafood menu is excellent. It also noted that while there are 'better and more varied cuts of meat in town,' BLT Prime

1 Geiling, Natasha. 'A Definitive History Of Trump Steaks™.' *Think Progress*, 4 Mar. 2016, thinkprogress.org/a-definitive-history-of-trump-steaks-e0e6fc31b689/.

is the only one that dry-ages its beef in lockers lined with pink Himalayan salt.[2]

Back at home in Trump Tower, though, the Trump Grill didn't fare as well. *Vanity Fair* said it 'could be the worst restaurant in America,' serving 'rich man slop.' A lunch there included:

'Flaccid, gray Szechuan dumplings with their flaccid, gray innards'
An 'Ivanka salad,' supposed to be Greek, with no olives
Disappointing cocktails that tasted like they had fruit concentrate; the reviewer and friends couldn't bring themselves to order Trump wine.

A Christmas decoration above their table fell on them as they ate. They also noticed that some of the signage was for the Trump 'Grille.' Trump Grill/Grille, *Vanity Fair* concluded, is meant for the 'hooded masses to visit once and never return.'[3]

In 2012, Trump's signature steakhouse in Las Vegas, DJT Steakhouse, was closed for earning a 'C' grade for health code violations. DJT was cited for *50 violations*. Among other problems, inspectors found month-old caviar, expired yogurt, five-month-old duck, two-week old tomato sauce, expired dressing, and an improperly functioning freezer.

Like Trump Steaks, DJT gets mixed reviews today. Yelpers give it three stars out of five and *Pace Vegas*, an online paper, ranks it among the 'five most disgusting restaurants' in town. Even Open Table only gives it 3.5 stars. But it's included in *Best of Vegas*.

2 Sietsema, Tom. 'BLT Prime Review: Trump Hotel's Steakhouse Does Plenty of Things Right.' *The Washington Post*, 14 Dec. 2016, https://goo.gl/3pJHcL.

3 Nguyen, Tina. 'Trump Grill Could Be the Worst Restaurant in America.' *Vanity Fair*, 25 May 2017, www.vanityfair.com/news/2016/12/trump-grill-review.

# 77. SOME BANKS STAY AWAY FROM TRUMP

In spite of his wealth and business success, most banks have stayed away from doing business with Trump over the past several years. Germany's Deutsche Bank is an exception.

According to a 2016 investigation by *Mother Jones*, Deutsche Bank has loaned the Trump Organization about $2.5 billion since 1998 and has committed to another $1 billion. As of 2016, he owed the bank more than $350 million.[1] It's like the bank and Trump are co-dependents, a situation that must make Angela Merkel and other EU nations even more nervous. (I know, this is not Britain's problem anymore.)

Why are other banks staying away from Trump? *The Street* says it's because of his 'business practices,'[2] which were not specified. *The Street* also says the employee orientation sessions at investment firm Goldman Sachs use Trump as an example of the kind of client to avoid.

Furthermore, six banking executives and attorneys who Trump asked for help as he faced multiple bankruptcies in 1990 spoke to Reuters about the differences in their recollections and Trump's version of events laid out in his book *The Art of the Comeback*.

Three stated that they summoned Trump to discuss debt restructuring—quite the opposite of his claim that he foresaw a downturn in the real estate market and called for meetings with the banks. All three say Trump didn't even realize how precarious his situation was until they reviewed his books and explained the situation to him. And, they emphasize, the terms of the deals they negotiated with him were dictated in the interest of their respective banks, not the Trump Organization, as he bragged in the book.

One credit specialist at a bank that had loaned a lot of money to Trump decided to revisit his loan portfolio after The Federal

1 Choma, Russ. 'Donald Trump's Giant Conflict of Interest Just Got Bigger.' *Mother Jones*, 23 June 2017, www.motherjones.com/politics/2016/09/donald-trump-and-deutsche-bank/.

2 Stewart, Emily. 'Troubled Deutsche Is One of the Few Banks That Still Lend Donald Trump Money.' *The Street*, 30 Sept. 2016, www.thestreet.com/story/13837506/1/troubled-deutsche-is-one-of-the-few-banks-that-still-lend-donald-trump-money.html.

Reserve, which is the US' central banking system, asked banks to review their real estate loans as the economy began to sink in 1989. The specialist considered Trump would almost certainly go bankrupt.

Trump's other lenders became aware of his financial straits when he drew down his entire $100 million line of credit in a single day from a bank now owned by...Deutsche Bank. A banker who had made loans to Trump's Atlantic City properties says that at this time, 'he was spending money like a drunken sailor.'[3]

The six bankers dispute Trump's account in his book that representatives from 72 banks capitulated to his terms for loan deferments or he would declare bankruptcy to 'tie you guys up for years.' While bankruptcy would have made it a little more difficult to collect from Trump, he actually had very little leverage. In addition, he had personally guaranteed many of the loans, which is probably why he sold the Trump Shuttle and personal property like his prized yacht.

The bankers gave him a monthly allowance of $450,000 to keep his operations going, but structured in a way that met their payment terms. 'We had to be sure he would pay attention,' one explained. 'We would meet with him every Friday morning.'[3]

3 'Trump Bankers Question His Portrayal of Financial Comeback.' *Fortune*, fortune.com/2016/07/17/trump-financial-comeback-story/.

## 78. THREE OF TRUMP'S TOP ATLANTIC CITY EMPLOYEES DIED IN A HELICOPTER CRASH

Nothing good came out of Trump's Atlantic City era. The casinos failed, leaving hundreds, if not thousands, of people without jobs. Vendors and contractors were unpaid for months and those who finally did get paid received pennies on the dollar.[1]

Tragically, three of Trump's most trusted employees died in a helicopter crash en route from New York to Atlantic City in October, 1989.

Stephen Hyde, who was president of the Trump Organization's Atlantic City operations; Mark Grossinger Ettis, President and COO of the Taj Mahal casino; Jonathan Benanav, executive vice president of the Trump Plaza Hotel & Casino and two crew all perished when a chartered helicopter split apart in mid-air.

Trump, according to biographers Kranish and Fischer, was devastated. The trio had helicoptered in from Atlantic City that morning to join Trump at a press conference for an upcoming boxing match promoted by Trump Sports and Entertainment. They missed the return flight back and hired a charter helicopter instead. They had no way of knowing that one of the rotor blades had a tiny scrape that would expand en route to southern New Jersey. A piece broke off, upsetting the helicopter's aerodynamics and resulting in a massive break that, as Kranish and Fischer write, 'rain[ed] wreckage' on the carriageway below.[2] Later, a government investigation concluded that the scratch occurred during manufacturing.

Trump called the families of the three men to break the news. Then he boarded a helicopter bound for Atlantic City to meet with employees and family members. The irony was not lost on him; John O'Donnell, the president of Trump Plaza Hotel & Casino and Benanav's boss told Kranish and Fischer that 'for the first time since I had known him, I heard fear and uncertainty in his voice.'[2]

---

1 Tully, Shawn. 'Donald Trump Got a Tax Break For Stiffing Contractors.' *Fortune*, 8 Oct. 2016, fortune.com/2016/10/08/donald-trump-taxes-contractors/.

2 Kranish and Fischer, *Trump Revealed*, 2016.

The following day, Trump met with more than 100 managers in a conference room. It's uncertain if he was supposed to be on the fatal flight; afterwards he told CNN that he was invited to go but was too busy. O'Donnell believed this was Trump trying to shift attention to himself.

Trump served as a pallbearer at Etis's funeral, which was attended by a thousand mourners. The next day, he went to Benanav's, where Marla Maples, who had been staying at the Atlantic City properties, was observed slipping into chapel. Ivana glared at her; 'I was sure she was going to throw a punch,' O'Donnell recalled.

At the third funeral for Hyde, O'Donnell said he watched Trump stare at a photo of the deceased man and saw a single tear slip down his face. 'For the first time, I saw sadness...profound sadness,' he said. Trump has said that the days following the deaths of the three men were the most difficult in his life, aside from the deaths of his brother Freddy and his parents.

# 79. TRUMP TAJ MAHAL HAD THE WORST OPENING WEEK EVER[1]

After the deaths of the Atlantic City executives, Trump decided that their grand project, the Trump Taj Mahal, would be a 'magnificent memorial to their memory.'

It wasn't meant to be.

Just before the grand casino opened, Marvin Roffman, a respected securities analyst for the gaming industry, told the *Wall Street Journal* that the Taj needed to gross $1.3 million each day just to break even. It would have to be the most successful casino ever to accomplish this. But New Jersey didn't have the market, he said, to sustain these kind of earnings, although he predicted that the excitement surrounding the Taj would provide a generous initial payout.

It just so happened that Roffman had a meeting with Robert Trump, the younger and usually softer-spoken Trump, the morning the *Journal* published the article. Roffman drove up, took in what 'a billion dollars can buy,' and found Robert, who was in a really bad mood. Robert screamed that Roffman had 'stabbed investors in the back.' He was hustled off the property by security guards as Robert shrieked 'Get the f—k off the property!'

It turned out Roffman was wrong about one thing: the casino began tanking almost from the start. The day after its opening, regulators from New Jersey's Casino Control Commission closed the slot machines after discovering an accounting error. This was a big deal because the Taj had 2,900 slot machines—the most in Atlantic City.

Commission director Deno Marino had personally warned Trump several months earlier that the Taj needed a larger 'hard count room,' the secure area where coins are tallied and sorted for the next day. The existing one was to small for the sheer number of slot machines. Trump assured the commissioner he would do this but never got around to it.

---

1 Kranish and Fisher, *Trump Revealed*, 2016.

Count-room workers were unable to keep up with the volume and the room became excruciatingly hot. Marino relaxed a rule and allowed the doors to stay open so that cooler air could get in. But the counters came up with a $220,000 undercount for the final tally. State law requires a balanced account, so the slot machines had to be closed until the error was resolved.

In his eleven years as commissioner, Marino told biographers Kranish and Fisher, he'd never encountered this problem.

Late on the third day, a counter stubbed his toe as he entered the room and discovered a bag holding $220,000 worth of tokens was being used to prop open the room's steel door.

Trump told the press that the slot machines were closed because workers were unable to keep up with the volume—a partial truth. *The New York Times* dutifully reported it.

In the meantime, Trump had informed Roffman's employer that he would sue unless Roffman was fired, which he was three days after the *Journal* article. To his credit, he successfully fought back for wrongful termination and received a $750,000 settlement from his former employer. Then he sued Trump as well and received an undisclosed settlement.

# 80. TRUMP WAS OBSESSED WITH BARACK OBAMA

Donald Trump has long been obsessed with President Barack Obama and has rarely missed a chance to insult him and/or question his legitimacy as the 44th President of the United States.

In 2008, Trump hijacked the so-called 'birther movement' that questioned and later challenged, President Obama's birthplace and whether he was born a US citizen. The US Constitution requires Presidents to be native born.

The turning point came in 2011, when the Trump-led birther movement was in full force. Trump attended the annual White House Correspondents' Dinner, an event in which a leading comedian lampoons the President and pretty much anyone else who's a bigwig in Washington. The President is expected to do the same, and Obama used the occasion to mock Trump, who had recently announced he wouldn't run for President in 2012. 'We all know your credentials and breadth of experience,' Obama said, and went on to tease Trump's leadership as demonstrated on *The Apprentice*.

Later, the Trump campaign falsely claimed the birther question was initially started by Hillary Clinton's 2008 campaign for President. In fact, it began in Illinois in 2003, when Obama prepared to run for Senate and an opponent, Andy Martin, called him a 'closet Muslim.'[1] That was enough to launch a thousand conspiracy theories.

Obama was, of course, born in Hawaii on August 4, 1961 to a US citizen and an African student residing in Hawaii on a student visa. Even if he had been born outside the US, his citizenship would have been assured by his having an American parent.

1 Cheney, Kyle, and Nick Gass. 'No, Clinton Didn't Start the Birther Thing. This Guy Did.' *Politico*, 16 Sept. 2016, www.politico.com/story/2016/09/birther-movement-founder-trump-clinton-228304.

# 81. TRUMP SET PRESIDENTIAL PRECEDENTS BY JUST *BECOMING* PRESIDENT

Trump's age at the time he became President and his lack of experience in public office set two new precedents for the American Presidency.

Donald Trump was 70 years old when he took the oath of office in January 2017. Previously, Ronald Reagan was the oldest President to do this when he took the oath of office in January 1981 at age 69.

In addition, Trump is the only US President who has never held public office or served in the armed forces. Presidents have served in Congress, as governors, in the military, as ambassadors, and as judges. In fact, many young men in years past with political ambition first sought military service—including George Washington himself.

Barack Obama, whose lack of experience many people questioned during his 2008 Presidential campaign, was a sitting Senator (albeit for just three years) when he declared his candidacy in February 2007. Prior to his election to the US Senate, Obama served seven years in the Illinois Senate, winning three elections.

Trump had flirted with Presidential campaigns many times. He discussed possibly running for President in 1988 during an appearance on Oprah Winfrey's chat show. He said he probably would not run because 'I love what I'm doing' but 'if it got so bad I would never want to rule it out totally,' adding, 'I think I'd win. I'd never go in it to lose.'[1] If he had run and won in 1988, he would have been the youngest President ever at age 42. As it stands, Theodore Roosevelt became the youngest person to assume the Presidency upon the assassination of William McKinley in 1901, just before his 43rd birthday.

In 2000, Trump actually entered the California presidential primary as a Reform Party candidate and won about 15,000 votes. 2000 was the year the US Supreme Court ultimately decided the

---

1 'Donald Trump Teases a Presidential Bid During a 1988 Oprah Show.' *YouTube*, uploaded by The Oprah Winfrey Show/OWN, 25 June 2015, https://www.youtube.com/watch?time_continue=157&v=SEPs17_AkTI

outcome of the election and declared Republican George W. Bush the winner.

In 2004, Trump again spoke about running for President. Perhaps it was a back-up plan in case *The Apprentice* didn't work out.

During the 2011 season of *Celebrity Apprentice*, Trump mentioned 'I'm thinking of running for President,' to the assembled celebrities. 'Do you think I'd make a good President?' Actor Gary Busey immediately burbled his enthusiasm. Trump was serious enough that he actually delayed renewing the show for another season in 2012.

Trump did consider a more conventional path to the Presidency in 2013, when he first met with several New York Republican leaders to discuss running for governor. Over the next several months, he flew around the state to attend rallies and speak with Republican activists, who were eager to find a strong challenger to Governor Andrew Cuomo. He soon lost interest as other New York Republicans began to voice their interest in the office as well.

## 82. TRUMP BREAKS RECORDS FOR LOW PUBLIC APPROVAL RATINGS

Trump's approval ratings fell faster than any other President since such polls started. Most polls agree he started out with approval ratings at about 49% when he was inaugurated in January 2017.

According to the research firm SSRS, by July, just 38% of 1,018 adult Americans surveyed approved of how he had been handling the presidency. Fully two-thirds said they didn't trust most of the communications from the White House (so much for 4 am tweeting) and 30% said they 'trusted nothing' they heard from that particular outlet.

By comparison, Barak Obama's approval rating was 51% and George W. Bush's was 56% at the six-month mark. Bill Clinton's was 44%, making Trump's rating a new record low.[1] Moreover, Trump's approval ratings have fallen in every state since he was elected, according to an October 2017 Morning Consult poll.

A majority of voters in half the states said they disapproved of Trump's job performance. Illinois, a state that went to Hillary Clinton, saw a 30% drop in approval, the largest in any state. But even so-called Red states that voted for Trump have seen massive drops in his approval, with a 23% drop in Tennessee and 21% in Mississippi.[2]

You can follow near-daily polls on Trump's approval ratings according to major polls on a site called FiveThirtyEight at https://projects.fivethirtyeight.com/trump-approval-ratings/. Here, you can also compare Trump's performance with previous presidents going back to Harry S Truman, who was in the White House from 1945–1953.

---

1 Agiesta, Jennifer. 'Poll: Declining Approval for Trump at 200 Days.' CNN, 8 Aug. 2017, www.cnn.com/2017/08/07/politics/poll-trump-approval-down-amid-distrust/index.html.

2 Easley, Cameron. 'Trump Approval Dips in Every State, Though Deep Pockets of Support Remain.' Morning Consult, 12 Oct. 2017, morningconsult.com/2017/10/10/trump-approval-dips-in-every-state-though-deep-pockets-of-support-remain/.

# 83. TRUMP MAY BE ENCOURAGING HIS PUBLIC PERCEPTION AS FLAKY

Rex Tillerson is one of the many millionaires and billionaires working in the Trump Administration. He takes his job as Secretary of State (a position Hillary Clinton held during the first Obama Administration) very seriously and he is not amused by the antics at the White House.

Tillerson came to the White House from his position as CEO of ExxonMobil, the world's largest oil company and the seventh richest company anywhere. He had never had another employer until he came to the White House.

By July, Tillerson had had enough of Trump's tweeting foreign policy announcements that directly contradicted official State Department policy that presumably had been approved by the White House. It's also a safe bet that Rex doesn't appreciate the 'help' from Jared Kushner, Trump's son-in-law, who has been given a foreign policy portfolio that includes Israel and Palestine. During a meeting with national security advisors that month, Tillerson was widely reported to have called the President 'a f—ing moron.'[1]

In October, another interesting story came out that speculated the President might be encouraging his staff to depict him as 'a crazy guy,' according to the news website Axios. (Axios might be branded as 'liberal' but its funding comes from sources across the political spectrum, including the ultra-conservative Koch Industries, PhRma, which represents pharmaceutical manufacturers, and Wal-Mart. Its founders are from Politico, which in turn was founded by former *Washington Post* editors.)[2]

Axios reporter Jonathan Swan reported that the President's advice to Robert Lighthizer, the US Trade Representative, as he prepared to discuss a free trade pact with South Korea was to tell

1 Filkins, Dexter. 'Rex Tillerson at the Breaking Point.' The New Yorker, The New Yorker, 11 Oct. 2017, www.newyorker.com/magazine/2017/10/16/rex-tillerson-at-the-breaking-point.
2 Swan, Jonathan. Scoop: Trump Urges Staff to Portray Him as 'Crazy Guy'. 1 Oct. 2016, www.axios.com/inside-trumps-crazy-train-2491643924.html.

them, '...if they don't give the concessions now, this crazy guy will pull out of the deal.'[2]

This came on the heels of a Trump tweet to Secretary Tillerson about avoiding a nuclear exchange with North Korea (kind of a big deal for those of us in the vicinity of California): 'Save your energy, Rex, we'll do what has to be done!'

I have to think Tillerson's dentist is busy making mouth guards to protect against teeth grinding.

There were earlier hints that Trump could be playing the role of a crazy man:

The 'Rocket Man' tweets and UN speech (see Fact #90)
Tweeting out threats to leave the North American Free Trade Agreement, which lets us get cheap beer from Canada and really good cooking vanilla from Mexico, among other things
Threatening to withdraw from NATO, which...well
Refusing to reassure NATO allies that the United States would defend them against an attack from Russia.

*Bloomberg*'s Hal Brands reminded his readers that during the 2016 campaign, Trump said 'we must, as a nation, be more unpredictable.' Brands optimistically hopes Trump is beginning to recognize that bluffing in business is different than bluffing with nuclear warheads.[3]

A small number of politicians have questioned if Trump really is 'crazy.' In July 2017, an open microphone caught Senators Susan Collins, a Republican from Maine, and Jack Reed, a Democrat from Rhode Island, discussing the US budget. Reed, speaking of the President, says, 'I think he's crazy,' and Collins replies, 'I'm worried.'[4]

3 Brands, Hal. 'Trump's Madman Theory Is Simply Crazy.' Bloomberg.com, Bloomberg, 10 Oct. 2017, www.bloomberg.com/view/articles/2017-10-10/trump-s-madman-theory-is-simply-crazy.
4 'Senators Caught on Hot Mic 'Worried' about 'Crazy' Trump.' *The Washington Post*, 25 July 2017, https://goo.gl/oYTN7v

## 84. TRUMP SPENT MUCH OF HIS FIRST SEVERAL MONTHS IN OFFICE LYING ABOUT THE SIZE OF HIS INAUGURATION CROWD

Trump falsely claimed that his Inauguration drew 1.5 million spectators, the largest in history. Experts think otherwise.

Presidents take the oath of office in front of the US Capitol Building, which faces the National Mall that stretches almost two miles to the steps of the Lincoln Memorial. Experts in crowd control and intelligence agreed that the Trump Inauguration had one of the lowest turnouts ever. But as we know, size really matters to Trump, whether it's his hands, his bank accounts, his home…his whatever.

The Washington Metro system showed much lower ridership on Trump's inauguration day—570,557—than for Obama's two inaugurations. In fact, the busiest day in Metro's history was on Obama's 2013 inauguration, when it reached 1.1 million bus and underground riders.

Metro's second-busiest day came the day after Trump's inauguration: the historic Women's March, which also took place on the National Mall. The transport number was also about 1.1 million on that day.[1]

Trump was so worked up over reports about the size of the Inauguration crowd that he actually complained about it on a visit to the Central Intelligence Agency, where he was supposed to try to backtrack uncomplimentary things he said on the campaign trail about US intelligence gathering. (A week earlier, he compared the CIA to Nazis.) Instead, he complained about journalists being 'among the most dishonest human beings on earth' and reiterated his claim that 1.5 million people attended.

In fact, it appears that there were at least as many people who came to Washington to protest against Trump as who came to cheer him on (or just to see an inauguration). It's not just the lying media who reported this; the *Washington Post* asked crowd scientists Marcel Altenburg and Keith Still of Manchester Metropolitan University to look at photos and video of the Inauguration and the Women's March.

1  Robertson, Lori, and Robert Farley. 'The Facts on Crowd Size.' FactCheck.org, 23 Jan. 2017, https://goo.gl/hv6ig2.

They estimated at least 470,000 people were at the Women's March at its peak, and about 160,000 for the Inauguration at its peak density.[2]

Professor Altenburg explained that from Trump's position, he would have only seen the tightly-packed front one-third of the crowd. He and Still looked at several live feeds from the day and concluded there were far fewer in the back. (Keep in mind that not everyone riding the Metro was attending an event, any event.)

Sean 'Spicey' Spicer, who served as Trump's press secretary from the transition period until he quit in July 2017, dutifully echoed his boss. 'This was the largest audience to ever witness an inauguration, period,' he squeaked. Spicer, who apparently had never attended an inauguration from the crowd point of view, falsely claimed that fences and metal detectors prevented people from getting to the Mall in time to see the swearing-in. But they had been used for Obama's inaugurations, which, after all, were protecting the first-ever black person elected President.[3] Spicer later explained that he included television and online viewing to back up his claim.

---

2  Wallace, Tim, and Alicia Parlapiano. 'Crowd Scientists Say Women's March in Washington Had 3 Times As Many People As Trump's Inauguration.' *The New York Times*, 22 Jan. 2017, www.nytimes.com/interactive/2017/01/22/us/politics/womens-march-trump-crowd-estimates.html?_r=0.

3  Qui, Linda. 'Donald Trump had biggest inaugural crowd ever? Metrics don't show it.' *Politifact*, 21 Jan. 2017, http://www.politifact.com/truth-o-meter/statements/2017/jan/21/sean-spicer/trump-had-biggest-inaugural-crowd-ever-metrics-don/.

# 85. TRUMP EXPECTS PERSONAL LOYALTY OVER SWORN OATHS TO SERVE THE NATION

Every person who works for the United States Government, from low-ranking civil servants to military personnel to Members of Congress and their staff, takes an oath that includes the words 'preserve, protect, and defend' the country. The President takes this oath as well; the actual words are provided in the Constitution.

Donald Trump views government employees as his own. He expects personal loyalty and went as far as to demand it from James Comey, the director of the Federal Bureau of Investigation (FBI).

Like most FBI directors, Comey kept his politics private. This is important because FBI directors are appointed by Presidents to serve ten-year terms that may be renewed by the next President. Comey's term began in 2013 when the Senate approved his nomination by President Obama.

So it wasn't surprising to notice Comey's discomfort when Trump sought to single him out during a photo session in the Oval Office with other high-ranking Administration officials. His body language said it all. Just a week later, he was invited to dine at the White House, alone with the President. During the meal, Comey later testified to the Senate, the President asked him if he wanted to keep his job.

'I need loyalty, I expect loyalty,' the leader of the free world said. Comey testified that he said he would provide honesty, to which Trump responded, 'honest loyalty.' Comey says he responded 'you will get that from me' but admits they may have had different ideas about what this means.[1]

Two weeks later, Trump summoned Comey to the Oval Office where he found a bunch of cronies Attorney General Jeff Sessions and other White House aides. Trump asked them to leave, which is a very unusual thing since Presidents rarely, if ever, meet alone with FBI directors. This is one way directors can remain above political influence.

DONALD TRUMP IN 100 FACTS

---

1 Schmidt, Michael S. 'In a Private Dinner, Trump Demanded Loyalty. Comey Demurred.' *The New York Times*, 11 May 2017, www.nytimes.com/2017/05/11/us/politics/trump-comey-firing.html.

Trump asked, or more likely, demanded, that Comey drop an investigation into Mike Flynn, a retired Army general who was the National Security Advisor for exactly 24 days until he was fired for lying to Vice President Mike Pence about his communications with the Russian ambassador. Flynn 'is a good guy and has been through a lot,' Trump told Comey. 'I hope you can let this go.'[2]

Don't think for a moment that Trump personally cared about Flynn. He had been worried for some time that he'd be dragged into the 'Russia investigation' even though Comey told him at least three times that he wasn't. Trump insisted in *nine* meetings that the FBI director needed to publicly state he wasn't under investigation because this was having a deleterious effect on his ability to lead the nation. (OK, maybe he didn't say deleterious.)[2]

Trump fired Comey on May 9, telling his buddies of the moment, who happened to be high-ranking Russian officials, that Comey was 'crazy, a real nut job,' adding 'I'm not under investigation.'[3] The letter firing Comey was sent to FBI headquarters; Comey, however, was in Los Angeles meeting with employees there. He learned of his firing from a television news alert.

2 Collinson, Stephen, et al. 'Comey: Trump Asked Me to Let Flynn Probe Go.' CNN, 8 June 2017, www.cnn.com/2017/06/07/politics/james-comey-testimony-released/index.html.

3 Apuzzo, Matt, Maggie Haberman and Matthew Rosenberg. 'Trump Told Russians That Firing "Nut Job" Comey Eased Pressure From Investigation.' *The New York Times*, 19 May 2017, www.nytimes.com/2017/05/19/us/politics/trump-russia-comey.html.

## 86. TRUMP DOESN'T UNDERSTAND THE DIFFERENCE BETWEEN A LAW AND AN EXECUTIVE ORDER

Sally Yates was a Deputy Attorney General who became the Acting Attorney General when Trump entered office. She devoted almost all her career to serving the US, first as an Assistant US Attorney for the Northern District of Georgia, where she prosecuted local cases in federal (US) court, including white collar fraud and political corruption.

During the Senate hearings that confirmed her appointment as Deputy Attorney General in 2015, Jeff Sessions (now the current Attorney General) asked her if she would disobey an unlawful order from the President. He warned her to 'watch out because people will be asking you to do things that you just need to say no about.'

'Senator,' Yates responded, 'I believe that the attorney general or deputy attorney general has an obligation to follow the law and the Constitution and to give their independent legal advice to the President.'[1]

On January 27, 2017, Trump issued an executive order banning citizens from seven Muslim countries from entering the US for 90 days. A federal judge in New York blocked the order a day later, and another in Massachusetts issued a temporary restraining order the day after that.

On January 29, Yates announced that she was instructing Justice Department lawyers not to defend Trump's order because this would run counter to the rulings and 'nor am I convinced that the Executive Order is lawful.' In other words, she was fulfilling her pledge to Senator Sessions.[2]

Trump fired her the next morning, with the White House issuing a statement saying she had 'betrayed the Department of

---

1  McKirdy, Euan. 'Sally Yates in 2015: AG Obligated to 'Follow the Law'.' CNN, 31 Jan. 2017, www.cnn.com/2017/01/31/politics/sally-yates-jeff-sessions-deputy-attorney-general-hearing/index.html.

2  Perez, Evan, and Jeremy Diamond. 'Trump Fires Acting AG after She Declines to Defend Travel Ban.' CNN, 31 Jan. 2017, www.cnn.com/2017/01/30/politics/donald-trump-immigration-order-department-of-justice/index.html.

Justice by refusing to enforce a legal order.' It also called her 'an Obama Administration appointee who is weak on borders and very weak on illegal immigration.' Yates' temporary replacement, Dana Boente, the US Attorney for the Eastern District of Virginia, was quoted as saying he would 'defend and enforce the laws of our country.'[2]

But an Executive Order isn't a law. Laws are passed by Congress and are part of the United States Code. Executive Orders aren't part of that code. Furthermore, Congress can override Presidential vetoes of laws they pass with a two-thirds vote for the law, but this doesn't work the other way around. The President cannot create a law, period.

Nor is an Executive Order 'a legal order' as the White House statement implied. An Executive Order can have the power of a law if it there is an actual law or Constitutional power behind it. But there was no such law, and the courts were clearly not convinced that this particular order had Constitutional backing.

This is all complicated, but that doesn't mean it should be glossed over. During the campaign, Trump (who is not a lawyer) made plenty of statements about 'illegal Executive Orders' made by President Obama. Some of Obama's Executive Orders were challenged in court, with parts held up and parts dismissed. Trump, however, appears to be under the illusion that the President is a kind of emperor with absolute authority. Anyone in his way is weak, un-American, or a loser.

# 87. TRUMP'S CABINET AND ADVISORS ARE A WHO'S WHO OF AMERICAN MILLIONAIRES AND BILLIONAIRES

In July 2017, *Forbes* calculated that members of Trump's Cabinet had an aggregate net worth of $4.3 billion dollars and included two fellow billionaires, Commerce Secretary Wilbur Ross (worth $2.5 billion) and Education Secretary Betsy DeVos (worth $1 billion).

There was one billionaire in Obama's outgoing Cabinet, Commerce Secretary Penny Pritzker, whose net worth was estimated to be $2.4 billion, just shy of her successor Wilbur Ross. Trump's Cabinet is packed with private sector CEOs who come from some of the wealthiest businesses in the US and in the world.

Secretary of State Rex Tillerson was CEO of ExxonMobil, where he spent his entire career before coming to the White House.

Defense Secretary James Mattis, a retired Marine Corps general, served on the board of military contractor General Dynamics.

Education Secretary Betsy DeVos married into the family that made a fortune with Amway.

Labor Secretary Andy Puzder grew the Hardee's and Carl's Jr. fast food chains

Commerce Secretary Wilbur Ross specialized in distressed assets and made his fortune merging companies from fading industries—steel, coal, textiles—and selling them for huge profits. Ross structured the deal that forced Trump to give up 50% of his stake in the Taj Mahal casino in Atlantic City in 1991 after his creditors realized he was on the verge of bankruptcy.

In all, five of Trump's 15 Cabinet members had no appreciable experience in public or military service before coming to office. DeVos was an activist in Michigan for private school vouchers, a scheme in which the state government underwrites private school tuition through vouchers. She earned no direct money through this activism.

The idea behind vouchers is to allow lower-income children to attend private school; that, in practice, simply undermines public (government) schools by removing badly-needed funds and sending them to for-profit or religious schools. DeVos' stated goal is to get Congress to approve a federal voucher program, and that would siphon even more funds from public schools, which educate nearly 51 million children,[2] about 90% of all school-aged children.[3]

In addition, Trump formed two advisory councils made up of top corporate executives: the Strategy & Policy Forum, and the Manufacturing Council, to advise him on various economic issues. They included fellow billionaires like Jamie Demon, CEO of JP Morgan Chase, General Electric chair Jeff Immelt, Merck & Co. CEO Kenneth Frazier, and Inge Thulin, CEO of 3M.

These advisors, and almost all of their fellow Forum or Council members, resigned one after another in the days following Trump's incomprehensible statements about the events in Charlottesville, Virginia. It *was* a relief to know that not all billionaires, including those affiliated with Trump, believe that white supremacists and neo-Nazis are basically cut from the same cloth as nonviolent protesters against racism.

1 Peterson-Withorn, Chase. 'The $4.3 Billion Cabinet: See What Each Top Trump Advisor Is Worth.' *Forbes* Magazine, 5 July 2017, https://goo.gl/YcnS7J

2 National Center for Education Statistics. 'Fast Facts: What are the new back to school statistics for 2017?' https://nces.ed.gov/fastfacts/display.asp?id=372

3 Kolko, Jed. 'Where Private School Enrollment is Highest and Lowest Across the U.S.' CityLab.com, 13 August, 2014, www.citylab.com/equity/2014/08/where-private-school-enrollment-is-highest-and-lowest-across-the-us/375993/.

## 88. TRUMP'S CABINET MEMBERS AND TOP ADVISORS SAY DISTURBING THINGS

If there's one thing Americans can agree on, it's that Trump's Cabinet members and top advisors have uttered some of the weirdest things to come out of the White House—and their boss does a pretty good job of it, too.

Ben Carson, the Secretary of Housing and Urban Development, briefly ran for the Republican nomination for President. Later, as Trump was considering him for a Cabinet position, he publicly stated that he would not join the Cabinet because he 'has no government experience.'[1] This apparently did not occur to him as he weighed a Presidential run. And yet here he is.

Actually, Carson, a neurosurgeon who wrote a best-selling autobiography about his rise from poverty, was kind of entertaining to listen to. Among the comments he made on the campaign trail and over the years are these aperçus:

The Great Pyramids were built to store grain.

Transgender bathrooms are a solution to America's bathroom obsession. 'It's not fair for them to make everybody else uncomfortable.'

The signatories to the Declaration of Independence from Great Britain 'had no federal experience.' There was no federal government as yet in 1776. If he was referring to government experience, several had served in their respective colony legislatures.

Asked if a shooting in Oregon would change his feelings on gun ownership, he responded that 'I never saw a body with bullet holes that was more devastating than taking the right to arm ourselves away.'[2]

DONALD TRUMP IN 100 FACTS

1 Megerian, Chris. 'Former Presidential Candidate Ben Carson Says He Won't Join Trump's Cabinet Because He Has No Government Experience.' *Los Angeles Times*, 15 Nov. 2016, www.latimes.com/nation/politics/trailguide/la-na-trailguide-updates-ben-carson-won-t-be-joining-donald-1479231990-htmlstory.html

2 Gass, Nick, et al. 'Ben Carson's 15 Most Controversial Quotes.' *Politico*, 6 Nov. 2015, www.politico.com/story/2015/10/ben-carson-controversial-quotes-214614.

Another Trump Cabinet member with some radical ideas is former Texas Governor Rick Perry, who, when asked how he would shrink the size of government during a debate in 2012, famously couldn't remember all the departments he would abolish if elected—including the one he now heads, the Department of Energy. Now that he understands that much of the Department's work involves maintaining the nation's nuclear stockpile, he doesn't think it should be abolished. At least he's capable of learning.

The Secretary of Labor, Andrew Puzder, owns the fast food chains Carl's Jr. and Hardees. In 2016, Carl's Jr. ran a series of frankly sleazy television commercials featuring scantily-clad celebrities like Kim ('the hot one') Kardashian, Paris Hilton, and Heidi Klum eating drippy hamburgers. There was some backlash from women and other groups, but the adverts, Puzder told Fox, saved the company. 'We got the attention of this demographic, young hungry guys.'[3] Later, he filmed a commercial with his son in which he apologized for the son's poor taste. Oscar Wilde bows.

Trump's ambassador to Israel, David Friedman, has repeatedly called American Jews who support a two-state solution to the Israel/Palestine situation 'worse than kapos.' Friedman also says Jews who support peace with Palestinians, such as the lobby group J Street and its backers, 'are just smug advocates of Israel's destruction.'[4]

3 Fernandez, Henry. 'Andrew Puzder: Carl's Jr. Racy Ads Saved the Company.' *Fox Business*, 9 Mar. 2017, www.foxbusiness.com/features/2017/03/09/andy-puzder-carl-s-jr-racy-ads-saved-company.html.
4 Friedman, David. 'Read Peter Beinart and You'll Vote Donald Trump.' *Israel National News*, 5 June 2016, www.israelnationalnews.com/Articles/Article.aspx/18828.

# 89. UNDER THE DONALD, WE HAVE AN ENVIRONMENTAL DESTRUCTION AGENCY

If there's one area where Trump's policies will have an immediate effect, it's the establishment of his Environmental Destruction Agency.

President Richard Nixon created the Environmental Protection Agency (EPA) in 1970 at a time when Congress listened to public concerns about the impact human activity has on the environment. Nixon, who was quite conservative for his day (today he'd probably be blasted as a left-winger), created the EPA through an Executive Order that was later ratified by Congress.

According to an archived page from the pre-Trump EPA website (accompanied by a warning that the content may no longer apply), Nixon created 'a strong, independent agency to establish and enforce environmental protection standards, conduct environmental research, assist in combatting environmental pollution, and develop and recommend new policies for environmental protection.'[1]

Indeed, much of this no longer applies under Trump and Scott Pruitt, his appointment as EPA Administrator. As Oklahoma's Attorney General, Pruitt sued the EPA at least 14 times to challenge standards that protect the environment including:

Cross-state air pollution, a standard the Supreme Court had already upheld

Limits to mercury and toxins in air

Safeguards against pollutants released when factories start up, shut down, or malfunction

Protecting scenic vistas in national parks and protected wildernesses

Clean air standards for oil and gas facilities

EPA's Clean Water Rule

And much, much more you can read about at the Environmental Defense Fund, http://www.edfaction.org/scott-pruitts-web-fundraising-and-lawsuits.

1 Lewis, Jack. 'The Birth of EPA.' *EPA*, Environmental Protection Agency, 6 Sept. 2016, archive.epa.gov/epa/aboutepa/birth-epa.html.

Since joining EPA, Pruitt, who does not believe that human activity adds to global warming, has been on a crusade to undo US participation in anything that recognizes global warming, including research and treaty agreements. He is also actively working to remove protections to US waters and the air. The latter, at least, has an immediate effect on the entire world. The reason? Environmental protections are 'bad for business and industry.'

Pruitt was behind Trump's withdrawing the US from the Paris Climate Agreement, the most inclusive global agreement on climate change. As a result, the US is the *only* nation that is not part of this effort. This also leaves China—the world's largest polluter—as the world leader on the environment. China's President, Xi Jingping, is quite serious (thank goodness) about reducing his own country's emissions. He's working closely with traditional US allies like Canada, Germany, and France.

Here are some of the ways Trump and Pruitt are working to worsen the environmental health of the US:

1. Dismissed half of the 18-members on the EPA's Board of Scientific Counselors who focused on environmental science and economics, hazardous waste management, and natural resources management in favor of appointing coal, gas, and oil industry representatives.
2. Removed the EPA's Climate Change website, now archived at https://19january2017snapshot.epa.gov/climatechange_.html.
3. Ended the Clean Power Plan that lowers carbon emissions by almost one-third by 2030 and end the 'war on coal.' At least this won't have much impact since few power companies are interested in investing or re-investing in coal.
4. Halted a study on the risks that mountaintop removal coal mines pose to nearby residents. Researchers at the University of West Virginia uncovered increased birth defects in these populations.
5. Ended flood standards accounting on sea level rise, which help predict the rise in sea level. This provided more accurate

assessments on floodplains, but that also acknowledges sea levels are rising, a key indicator of global warming.

6. Presently delaying and working to eliminate tightened ozone standards.

7. Cancelled rules to protect whales from getting entangled in fishing nets.

8. Downsized the Bears Ears National Monument in Utah's Red Rock Country, which also holds protected ancient tribal artifacts from looting and destruction.

## 90. TRUMP MADE THE ONLY SPEECH IN UN HISTORY THAT INVOLVED ACTUAL SCHOOLYARD NAME-CALLING

On September 19, 2017, Trump addressed the United Nations and did something no other world leader had done at this forum: he called another world leader a name in the spirit of schoolyard bullying—something in which he does excel.

I am referring to Trump's labelling of the North Korean leader Kim Jong Un as 'Rocket Man.' He had already introduced the snipe on Twitter, his preferred way to communicate with the American public, foreign leaders, Cabinet members, Members of Congress… pretty much anyone involved with US laws and policies.

In verbally confronting 'a small group of rogue regimes that violate every principle on which the United Nations is based,' Trump discussed the regime's recent missile tests, including one that had just flown over Japan. He referred to Otto Warmbier, a young American imprisoned in North Korea for 17 months before he was returned to the US in 2017 in a coma, dying just a few days later. He made a rather opaque reference to the 1977 kidnapping of Megumi Yokota, a Japanese teenager abducted by a North Korean agent. (North Korea has admitted kidnapping at least 17 Japanese citizens in the late 1970s and early 1980s to help them train spies. It says Yokota died in captivity but her family believes she is still alive.)

'Rocket Man,' Trump declared, 'is on a suicide mission for himself and for his regime. The United States is ready, willing and able [to totally destroy North Korea], but hopefully this will not be necessary.'[1]

This kind of talk nearly tops another bizarre UN incident in 1960, when Soviet Union Premier Nikita Khrushchev called the Philippines' delegate, Lorenzo Sumulong, 'a jerk' and a 'toady of American Imperialism.' At one point, Khrushchev removed what

---

1 'Remarks by President Trump to the 72nd Session of the United Nations General Assembly.' The White House, 19 Sept. 2017, www.whitehouse.gov/the-press-office/2017/09/19/remarks-president-trump-72nd-session-united-nations-general-assembly.

appeared to be his right shoe and used it to gesture angrily toward the Philippine delegation. Some eyewitnesses claim he also banged his shoe on the podium.

Certainly, this is how it's been portrayed in the US. It makes you wonder if a young Donnie Trump had visited the UN that very day, perhaps on a school trip with the New York Military Academy.

After the Tweets and the UN address, many people recalled Elton John's song 'Rocket Man.' According to *The Washington Post*, online searches for 'Rocket Man' jumped from 400 per day to 4500 per day. This did not put it back on the Billboard tracks, but it did improve viewership of the official 'Rocket Man' video on Sir Elton's YouTube channel.[2] It's a sobering animated depiction by artist Majid Adin's of his own experience fleeing Iran.

For his part, Kim Jong Un now calls Trump a 'mentally deranged US dotard.'[3]

2  Bump, Philip. 'Analysis | Trump's 'Rocket Man' Fixation Doesn't Seem to Be Doing Much for Elton John.' *The Washington Post*, 19 Sept. 2017, www.washingtonpost.com/news/politics/wp/2017/09/19/trumps-rocket-man-fixation-doesnt-seem-to-be-doing-much-for-elton-john/?utm_term=.0cbf1541d25b.
3  Griffiths, James. 'What Is a 'Dotard'?' CNN, 23 Sept. 2017, www.cnn.com/2017/09/22/asia/north-korea-dotard/index.html.

# 91. TRUMP AND HIS STAFF CREATE 'ALTERNATIVE FACTS'

Perhaps no one in the Trump camp has made as many bizarre statements as Kellyanne Conway, Trump's campaign manager and now Counselor to the President. She specializes in misleading, misinformed, and plain old false statements.

Just after Trump's inauguration, Conway defended statements made by Sean 'Spicy' Spicer, then the White House Press Secretary, regarding the size of the crowd attending the Trump inauguration (see Fact #84) on the public affairs program *Meet the Press*. Spicer, she said, was giving 'alternative facts.' The program host, Chris Todd, responded 'Look, alternative facts are not facts. They're falsehoods.'

In February 2017, Conway defended Trump's immigration ban (later overturned by two federal courts) on the MSNBC program *Hardball* by referring to the 'Bowling Green Massacre.' Bowling Green is a tranquil town in Kentucky with a lovely state university of the same name. No massacre has ever taken place there. The following day, Conway explained that she was referring to the arrest of two Iraqi refugees in Bowling Green who had pleaded guilty to carrying out and supporting attacks on American soldiers in Iraq. No information has ever been released to suggest they were plotting an attack within the US.

Speaking of Spicey, his successor, Sarah Huckabee Sanders, is admirably unashamed to parrot untruths and attack reporters at press briefings for doing things like ask questions about statements that come out of the White House. In late October, Trump's Chief of Staff John Kelly was speaking on Fox News about decisions to remove Confederate monuments. He attributed 'the lack of an ability to compromise' as a cause for the Civil War. Not slavery, but a lack of compromise. A couple of days later, Sanders defended Kelly's statements in the White House Press room: 'All leaders are flawed.'

Another fake news piece came from the White House social media director Dan Scavino, Jr, who tweeted out a video from the President's and Vice President's Twitter accounts of a flooded

Miami International Airport during Hurricane Irma. It turns out the footage wasn't that airport, or even that hurricane. The airport's own Twitter account simply replied, 'This video is not from Miami International Airport.' Scavino deleted the tweets but did not apologize.

Of course, staff are learning from the master. For example, crime is one of Trump's favorite topics, but the information he tweets about it and offers at rallies is false. He often says murder is higher than ever in the US. (He does not support any kind of restriction on obtaining guns and ammunition.) But FBI statistics show falling murder rates every year since 2009. Murder rates reached their worst heights in 1980 and 1991.

Early in his Administration, on 2 February 2017, Trump told us to 'look what's happening last night in Sweden. Sweden, who would believe this?' Apparently, Trump thought there was a terrorist attack the previous night in Sweden but none was reported.

## 92. TRUMP TOLD AT LEAST ONE LIE PER DAY DURING HIS FIRST 40 DAYS IN OFFICE

Trump lied so often during his first several weeks in office that his staff and Congressional Republicans often explained to the public that we shouldn't take everything he says literally. Literally, they said this.

*The New York Times* has been tracking these lies since 21 January, the day after Trump took office. Here are some of the highlights from those first 40 days:

21 January: 'I wasn't a fan of Iraq. I didn't want to go to Iraq.' (He initially supported the invasion, as *Politico*, *The Washington Post*, FactCheck.org, and other sites have documented.)

25 January: 'Take a look at the Pew reports [on voter fraud].' The author of a 2012 report on voter fraud for the highly regarded Pew Research Center tweeted that voter integrity in the 2016 election was stronger than ever before.

3 February: Trump complained about 'professional anarchists, thugs and paid protesters' at rallies and counter-rallies. There is no evidence that any protesters at anti-Trump marches and other events were paid.

6 February: 1. '[Terrorism has] gotten to the point where it is not even being reported.' There is no sane way to answer this other than head-to-keyboard. 2. 'The failing @nytimes was forced to apologize to its subscribers for the poor reporting it did on my election win.' *The Times* never apologized for this. 3. 'The previous Administration...created a vacuum, ISIS was formed.' ISIS has been around since 2004, four years before Obama took office.

6 February: 'I have already saved more than $700 million. I got involved in negotiation on a fighter jet, the F-35.' The Department of Defense announced the F-35's price drop before Trump took office.

16 February: 'I guess it was the biggest Electoral College win since Ronald Reagan.' False; George H W Bush, Bill Clinton, and Barack Obama all had more Electoral College votes than Trump.

18 February: 'There was no way to vet those people [immigrants]. There was no documentation. There was no nothing.' Actually, the process to allow immigrants to remain in the country legally can take up to two years.

24 February: 'Obamacare covers very few people.' 20 million previously uninsured people than ever were able to obtain health insurance under the Affordable Care Act, also known as Obamacare.

28 February: 'We have begun to drain the swamp of government corruption by imposing a five-year ban on lobbying by executive branch officials.' The rule forbids lobbying their own agency— former Executive Branch employees can still lobby.

3 March: 'It's pathetic that the Dems have still not approved my full Cabinet.' He hadn't submitted paperwork on two candidates at that point.

4 March: 'Terrible: Just found out that Obama had my "wires tapped" in Trump Tower. Nothing found. This is McCarthyism!' This is true—nothing was found to indicate any wire tapping of Trump's home. Trump kept up this claim for a few weeks.

You can read more of this at https://www.nytimes.com/interactive/2017/06/23/opinion/trumps-lies.html?_r=0.

# 93. AMERICA'S POLITICAL DIVIDE GREW MARKEDLY DURING TRUMP'S FIRST YEAR IN OFFICE

It was no surprise to read an October 2017 report from the Pew Research Center that Republicans and Democrats grew further apart on basic political opinions than ever before during the Obama Administration. This gap grew at a rapid clip during the first several months of Trump's presidency.

Government assistance to the needy: 71% of Democrats and those who lean toward the party support more government assistance to the needy. Only 24% of their Republicans counterparts feel the same say.

Government is wasteful and inefficient: 69% of Republicans agree with this statement versus 45% of Democrats.

Racial discrimination prevents economic progress for blacks: Overall, 41% of Americans believe this is the primary reason that blacks have not progressed economically. But Republicans and Democrats differ on this by a margin of 50%. 64% for Democrats agree on this versus 14% of Republicans.

Is there discrimination? 63% of Republicans and those leaning this way say people see discrimination where it doesn't exist. 79% of Democrats disagree and believe just the opposite.

Obstacles to women's progress: 73% of Democrats and Democratic-leaning people say women continue to face significant obstacles to getting ahead, while 63% of their Republican counterparts say these obstacles are mostly gone. 70% of Republican men say obstacles women used to face are largely gone versus 65% of Democratic men. 53% of Republican women say women face fewer obstacles versus 79% of Democratic women.

Immigration: Almost two-thirds of Americans say immigrants bring hard work and talent and strengthen the country. 26% say they are a burden who 'take our jobs, housing and health care.'

84% of Democrats share positive views on immigrants, versus 42% of Republicans.

Accepting of LGB Americans: 70% of Americans accept homosexuality in our society, the highest percentage ever. This breaks down to include 54% of Republicans and 83% of Democrats.

Hard work gets people ahead: Less than half of Democrats (49%) say most people will get ahead by hard work alone. But 77% of Republicans say hard work pays off for most people.

People strongly dislike the other party: 44% of Democrats and those leaning this way have a very unfavorable opinion of Republicans, and 45% of Republicans and those leaning Republican return the favor.

Belief that Islam encourages violence: 65% of Republicans agree with this versus 25% of Democrats. Overall, almost half of all Americans (49%) say the religion doesn't encourage violence any more than other religions.

Republicans and Democrats don't even want to live in the same places! 65% of Republicans want to live in big houses on large lots far from shopping and schools. 61% of Democrats prefer smaller homes within walking distance of schools and shopping.[1]

In an interview with *The Atlantic*, Jocelyn Kiley, a Pew associate director of research, said the data show the extent of how the political divide apply to 'ostensibly' nonpolitical decisions like where to live. 'That reflects a lot about the state of the American political landscape right now.'[2]

1 Smith, Samantha. 'Government, Regulation and the Social Safety Net.' Pew Research Center for the People and the Press, 5 Oct. 2017 www.people-press.org/2017/10/05/2-government-regulation-and-the-social-safety-net/.
2 Foran, Clare. 'America's Political Divide Intensified During Trump's First Year as President.' *The Atlantic*, 5 Oct. 2017, www.theatlantic.com/politics/archive/2017/10/trump-partisan-divide-republicans-democrats/541917/.

# 94. TRUMP IS STRESSING AMERICA OUT

Donald Trump is stressing out his fellow Americans. You hear this from ordinary people, news addicts, and even children far too young to vote.

In August. 2017, the *New York Daily News* reported on something called 'President Trump Stress Disorder.' Staff writer Megan Cerullo spoke with therapists who report patients with new symptoms like insomnia, hyper vigilance, and an 'inability to pull themselves away from the 24-hour news cycle' which no doubt adds to any stress. 'I have people I have not seen in literally 30 years that have called me to come back because of trauma,' one therapist told Cerullo. 'I am more than full. I am overworking.'

Some cited Trump's initial reluctance to condemn violence in Charlottesville, Virginia in August 2017 after 'Unite the Right' events. White supremacists held a torchlight march reminiscent of Ku Klux Klan rallies and attacked counter-protestors the following day. One woman was struck and killed by a car driven by a so-called 'alt-right activist.' Trump declared there were good people 'on both sides.' However, only one side actually attacked and successfully killed a person.

Talkspace, an online therapy service, reported its January traffic was three times higher than normal, and remained about 1.5 times higher as the year wore on.[1]

In November 2017, the American Psychological Association released a survey that found almost 60% of 3,400 adults it spoke to felt the US was at its lowest point that they could recall—even those who remember World War II and Martin Luther King Jr's assassination. Americans' stress is even higher today than it was after the September 11, 2001 terrorist attacks.[1] The survey did not mention Trump by name.

Earlier, in June, *The New England Journal of Medicine*, one of the world's premier medical journals, reported that 'events linked

---

1 Cerullo, Megan. 'How to Cope with President Trump Stress Disorder.' *NY Daily News*, 16 Aug. 2017, www.nydailynews.com/news/politics/cope-president-trump-stress-disorder-article-1.3414933.

to the recent presidential campaign and election have given rise to fear and anxiety in many Americans.'[2]

The authors, who come from the Harvard School of Public Health and McLean Hospital, a psychiatric hospital affiliated with Harvard Medical School, cited a widely reported national survey of 2000 teachers in which more than half said that their students felt emboldened to use racial and ethnic slurs. Another two-thirds (67%) said their students who were Muslim, immigrants, or children of immigrants expressed fears about what might happen to their families after the election. Even black children who were born US citizens worried that there might be a return to slavery or that they would be sent 'back to Africa.'[2]

They also reviewed earlier studies that indicate people who live in communities where prejudices are freely expressed are literally stressed into a higher risk for heart disease, particularly black residents. People who identify as LGBT and live in areas with high rates of anti-gay sentiment are three times more likely to die sooner than their counterparts in more accepting communities.

Community clinicians who work with immigrant communities are reporting more cases of anxiety, depression, and panic attacks.

2 Williams, David R, and Morgan Medlock. 'Health Effects of Dramatic Societal Events – Ramifications of the Recent Presidential Election.' *New England Journal of Medicine*, 8 June 2017, www.nejm.org/doi/full/10.1056/NEJMms1702111.

## 95. THERAPISTS HAVE DEVISED COPING MECHANISMS FOR TRUMP STRESS SYNDROME

Fortunately, America's therapists have responded to patients' anxieties and shared five coping techniques with *Daily News* readers. Many of them are pretty standard recommendations for stress and anxiety in general; it's just that the focus of a lot of Americans' stress is also included in these recommendations.

First, unplug from the news and social media at least for a few hours a day and certainly by 10 pm. 'It's just too agitating if you are anxious,' one says. This includes any political conversations. 'It's important to stay informed and to know your limits...give yourself a break,' said one psychologist with a busy practice in Washington, DC.

Second, get involved and take some positive action that will help regain a sense of empowerment. This generally means getting involved with organizations that support causes the patient believes in. Calling, writing, and emailing congressional and state representatives is another good method.

Third, exercise. If nothing else, it distracts from politics and social media. 'Run, swim, do push-ups, sit-ups, or [hoover] to Aretha Franklin,' one therapist said. Bonus: Aretha sang at President Obama's first inaugural.

Fourth, try to be understanding. Try to understand Trump's appeal and don't write off all his supporters as bigoted or ignorant people (difficult as that might be). We still have to live together.

Fifth, get professional help if your friends are sick of listening to you! Some things are beyond what a bestie, spouse, or partner can do for you.

The American Psychological Association (APA) offers additional suggestions:

Appreciate your ability to cope. We tend to underestimate our own resilience and problem-solving skills when we are stressed. Think about times when you overcame earlier obstacles that seemed nearly as hopeless, if not more so.

Write out your anxieties and assign a probability index from 1-10 with 10 being the most likely to happen. Since anxiety rests on the unknowns, remember that 'there are always possibilities,' as Mr. Spock liked to say. (The APA did not quote Spock but should have.)

Keep hope alive! (The APA actually said 'retain hope' but this refrain from Jesse Jackson's 1980s campaigns may resonate for some. Plus it's fun to talk like Rev. Jackson.) Reevaluate what's most important for you, your loved ones, and your community. Careful reevaluation can result in 'a course of meaningful behavior based on our deepest values.'

The APA also mentions that people it surveyed are coping through the times through prayer, listening to music, and meditation.

Other coping mechanisms include understanding that you can't control what goes on in Washington, DC (beyond voting, attending Town Halls, and communicating with representatives) but you can control how you behave. If thinking about President Trump makes you anxious, you can take a Trump Anxiety Test here: https://www.calmclinic.com/anxiety-test/

## 96. WHITE HOUSE STAFF TURNOVER IS CONSIDERABLE, BUT NOT RECORD-BREAKING

If you think there's been a lot of turnover in Trump's cabinet and White House staff, you're correct. It's been chaotic there at times, particularly compared to his two predecessors.

Looking at Trump's first six months in office, you do see more turnover in key roles like Chief of Staff, Communications Director, and Press Secretary. These are Presidential appointments, and do not need Senate approval and hearings like Cabinet nominations.

Trump's first Chief of Staff, Reince Priebus, held on to his job for just under seven months after losing a power struggle with Trump advisor and alt-right daddy Stephen Bannon. By contrast, Obama's stayed on for more than a year and a half and Bush's remained on the job for five years.

Trump went through three communications directors in his first six months. His first director, Michael Dubke, stayed longer than Obama's, Ellen Moran, who left after a few months to accept a position as chief of staff for the Secretary of Commerce. Bush's first director, Karen Hughes, held the job for eight months. Trump's second communications director, Anthony Scaramucci, triggered the resignation of his press secretary, Sean Spicer, who had actually held the job alongside his very public one. Scaramucci was fired after just 10 days.

Although the Communications Director oversees the Press Secretary, it's the latter that gets all the glory and/or mockery depending on performance. As we noted, Spicey stormed out after six and a half months. Obama's first press secretary stayed on for just over two years, while Bush's stayed for two-and-a-half years.

The National Security Advisor is another important position that almost mirrors Cabinet responsibilities but does not require Senate hearings and approval. Trump's first NSA advisor, Michael Flynn, resigned after just 24 days having admitted he lied to Vice President Mike Pence about his involvement with Russian officials. Obama's NSA remained with him for more than two-and-a-half years, while Bush's stayed for the entire first term.

DONALD TRUMP IN 100 FACTS

Presidents appoint FBI Directors for ten-year terms. Obama appointed James Comey, who Trump fired over the Russia investigation. He is only the second President to fire an FBI director; Bill Clinton fired his after he lost confidence in him during a 1993 ethics investigation. In both cases, these were directors who were in place when a new Administration came in and were fired during the President's first year in office.

Cabinet members must be approved by the Senate and are subjected to hearings to feel out their positions. Their turnover is usually lower than White House staff. So far, Trump has fired two cabinet members—Comey and the Acting Attorney General, Sally Yates, who refused to enforce the Muslim ban. There are persistent rumors that he will fire his chosen Attorney General, Jeff Sessions, for appointing a Special Counsel to look into Russian collaboration who is actually doing the job.

Both Obama and Bush fired Cabinet members. Notably, Obama fired Michael Flynn, then Director of the Defense Intelligence Agency, for sharing sensitive information with foreign intelligence officers without proper authorization. He warned Trump about bringing Flynn back to the White House.

# 97. TRUMP'S SPEECHES OFTEN VEER OFF TOPIC

One thing about attending or tuning into a Trump speech: you never really know what he's going to talk about. The posted topic may be quickly thrown aside.

Part of this is his tendency to ad-lib remarks, which can easily lead to another topic. Most of the time, this is tolerated but in September 2016, a pastor in Flint, Michigan caused a stir when she interrupted the Republican candidate to ask him to stick to topics they had agreed he would discuss.

One of Trump's more bizarre performances came during Black History Month in February 2017. A select group of black leaders were invited to the White House for a 'listening session.' Trump asked everyone to introduce him or herself and proceeded not to listen but inject his own opinions on topics that had nothing to do with black history. After saying he doesn't watch 'fake news' (his tag for CNN), he called out one of its regulars, Paris Denard, for 'working in a very hostile community.' He also praised and thanked Fox News: 'Fox has treated me very nice.'

He rejected a suggestion from radio host Armstrong Williams that some media try to be fair and objective. 'A lot of the media is actually the opposition party,' he complained. 'They're so biased and really is a disgrace [sic].'

Trump was also angry that 'they' (he didn't identify who) said he had removed a statue of Martin Luther King Jr from his office. 'It was a disgrace but that is how the press is.'[1]

Then there was the speech to the Boy Scouts Jamboree. Normally, this speech encourages Scouts to continue their work. Obama, for example, mentioned that 11 of the 12 men who walked on the moon were Scouts. He discussed the Scouts' long history of service for events like food drives for the poor and other volunteer work.

---

1 'Remarks by President Trump in African American History Month Listening Session.' The White House, 1 Feb. 2017, www.whitehouse.gov/the-press-office/2017/02/01/remarks-president-trump-african-american-history-month-listening-session.

George W Bush, who attended a Jamboree with temperatures that soared over 100°F, thanked the Scouts for their volunteer work and noted former Scouts who were in his Administration. He talked about how his mother served as his troop's Den Mother. He spoke about helping others in need.

When Donald Trump spoke to the Scouts, he talked about the Republican convention, the election, questioned if Obama had ever attended a Jamboree, mentioned a cocktail party he'd attended where he saw a once-famous businessman who lost everything, and told the Scouts it would be ok to say 'Merry Christmas.'

The Scouts, it was reported, listened politely.

What's going on here? Some people suggest Attention Deficit Disorder. As many have observed, he has a short attention span, shows impulsive behavior, is restless, and seems to get a real charge from social media. Look at how NATO leaders worked to ensure Trump wouldn't get bored at his first summit in May 2017. As one person who prepared the summit told *Foreign Policy*, 'It's like preparing to deal with a child—someone with a short attention span and mood who has no knowledge of NATO, no interest in in-depth policy issues, nothing. They're freaking out.'[2]

2 Gramer, Robbie. 'NATO Frantically Tries to Trump-Proof President's First Visit.' Foreign Policy, 15 May 2017, foreignpolicy.com/2017/05/15/nato-frantically-tries-to-trump-proof-presidents-first-visit-alliance-europe-brussels/.

# 98. AT LEAST FIVE WORLD LEADERS ARE MORE DISLIKED IN THEIR COUNTRIES THAN TRUMP

It could be worse: at least Trump isn't the head of Venezuela, Brazil, South Africa, Malaysia, or Greece. The leaders of these countries are even more disliked by the populace than Trump is in the US.

President Nicolas Maduro of Venezuela is probably the most disliked leader of his own people. He did inherit a mess from his predecessor, Hugo Chavez, who at least had enough magnetism to distract most people from Venezuela's considerable problems. Maduro has relied on police and the National Guard to control near-daily street protests. The problems stem from Venezuela's oil-dependent economy. Since the price of oil dropped, Venezuela cut support for social programs. Things didn't get better when Maduro tried to abolish the National Assembly in favor of a 'constituent assembly' to draw a new Constitution. (It's easy to imagine how Trump would *love* to do this.) Meanwhile, *Time* reports that almost three-quarters of Venezuelans have lost nearly 20 pounds due to food shortages.[1]

Brazil's President Michel Temer, who came to office after his predecessor was impeached, isn't doing much better with approval ratings in the single digits.[2] A good chunk of his cabinet is facing corruption charges in a national 'car wash' scandal along with dozens of legislators. Temer himself is facing an investigation into the claim he tried to bribe another politician. At least Trump doesn't bribe other people; he simply bullies them.

Jacob Zuma, President of South Africa since 2009, has an approval rating of 20%, and about 70% of South Africans want him to resign, according to politicsweb. The nation's currency has lost a third of its value during his presidency. Zuma is also facing about 800 charges. He is reportedly grooming his ex-wife

---

1 Bremmer, Ian. 'Venezuela's President Nicolas Maduro Is Toast: 5 Reasons Why.' *Time*, 11 Aug. 2017, time.com/4897084/venezuela-nicolas-maduro-borrowed-time/.

2 Watts, Jonathan. 'Brazilians Sick of Corrupt Politicians Hit the Streets to Protest Austerity Measures.' *The Guardian*, 28 Apr. 2017, www.theguardian.com/world/2017/apr/28/brazil-corruption-unions-strike-michel-temer-austerity.

to succeed him.[3] Marla Maples stays pretty private about her political interests, and while it's not unfathomable to imagine Ivana Trump's interest, she isn't a natural-born US citizen and is therefore ineligible to run for President.

Malaysia's Prime Minister Najib Razak, who visited the White House in 2017, is apparently surviving in office because he's allowing Sharia law to flourish in his country. Someone discovered $1 billion in his personal bank account, which he first claimed was a 'donation' from the Saudi royal family that he's since (mostly) returned. Malaysia was not on Trump's Asia itinerary for his two-week trip two months after the discovery.

Like Venezuela's Maduro, Greece's Prime Minister Alexis Tsiparis inherited a messy economy choking on austerity that hurt the worst-off. Tsiparis, who was elected in 2014 for promising to get German bankers to back off on demanding loan paybacks, hasn't 'Made Greece Great Again.' Tsiparis, who has a lot of street cred for being anti-authoritarian and all that, has done just what his predecessors have done: pushed through more austerity measures on an already exhausted populace, but without much public dissent. The Greeks, whose philosophical ancestors created democracy, are probably just as sick of politics as anyone else.

---

3 'Zuma`s Approval Rating Drops to New Lows in Metros.' Politicsweb, 5 Apr. 2017, www.politicsweb.co.za/documents/zumas-approval-rating-drops-to-new-lows-in-metros-.

## 99. TRUMP USES TWITTER FOR EVERYTHING FROM ATTACKING ENEMIES TO ANNOUNCING NEW POLICIES

Twitter is Trump's main communications tool and weapon.

He first started tweeting @realDonaldTrump in April 2009 and sent his first tweet in May to announce his upcoming appearance on the *Late Show with David Letterman*. It didn't take long for him to use Twitter to promote *The Apprentice*, his books, and quotes. It's possible these inoffensive tweets were from his staff.

*The Guardian* points to June 2011 as a turning point in Trump's tweets, when they became more political. It's also when his account went into overdrive, going up from perhaps 150 tweets a year to more than 100 per month.

When you think about it, Twitter is a perfect medium for Trump. It feeds the need for instant gratification and lets him engage at very high levels with celebrities and politicians he dislikes, and allows him to engage in 'casual cruelty,' as *The New York Times* aptly noted in 2015.[1] For example, a Tweet insulting the elderly actress Kim Novak backfired and, he admitted to the *Times,* 'I would have preferred I didn't send it. That was done in fun, but sometimes you do things in fun and they turn out to be hurtful, and I don't like doing that.'

By the time he announced his run for the Presidency, he was a true Twitter master. According to the *Times*, he was mentioned in 6.3 million Twitter conversations in just two months in 2015, dwarfing talk about his Republican rivals. He words were retweeted twice as often as Hillary Clinton and 13 times more often than the once-presumed nominee, Jeb Bush.

As a candidate, Trump used Twitter to create divisions within the American electorate as skillfully as Russians on Facebook. While he used the 'us versus them' as themes for his rallies,

DONALD TRUMP IN 100 FACTS

---

1 Barbaro, Michael. 'Pithy, Mean and Powerful: How Donald Trump Mastered Twitter for 2016.' *The New York Times*, 5 Oct. 2015, www.nytimes.com/2015/10/06/us/politics/donald-trump-twitter-use-campaign-2016.html.

189

on Twitter, 'them' became anyone who opposed his candidacy. 'Stupid,' 'weak,' and 'horrible' became trademarks, along with his favorite close, 'Sad!'

Since becoming President, Trump has continued to use Twitter to attack his enemies, usually Democrats, but also to announce major policy changes, often to the surprise of his own staff and Cabinet, not to mention Congressional Republicans.

He ordered the Department of Defense to reverse its order to allow transgendered people to serve in the military, catching the generals off-guard.

He twice tweeted out that Secretary of State Rex Tillerson should stop behind-the-scenes talks with North Korea. Tillerson was 'wasting his time trying to negotiate with Little Rocket Man (North Korean leader Kim Jong-un)...save your energy, Rex, we'll do what needs to be done!'

He has used Twitter to obliquely threaten North Korea, which has nuclear weapons, prompting Twitter to agree to revisit its policies on newsworthiness. While it could be argued that anything the President of the United States says is newsworthy, the platform is also concerned that his penchant for insulting, degrading, and ridiculing others may violate its own standards.

# 100. TRUMP'S 2018 VISIT TO GREAT BRITAIN WILL BE 'YOOG!'

Buckle your seat belts and lock up your dogs—Donald Trump is coming to visit Great Britain in 2018. It will be a 'yoog' success, probably the best visit you'll ever have had from someone so famous and successful.

Besides, we Americans need a break.

It won't be a state visit complete with meeting the Queen and addressing Parliament. Instead, it will likely be a fairly low-key event where Trump will, among other things, open the new US Embassy and visit his good friend, Ambassador Robert Wood ('Woody') Johnson IV (introduced in Fact #52).

In fact, it's a good bet that Trump won't meet with anyone with royal blood flowing in his or her veins. Prince Charles, who has a long history of environmental activism, was 'in a diplomacy row' with Trump in 2017, according to *The Independent*. Charles, the paper says, would be happy to pass Trump along to one of his sons.[1]

But that may not work out, either. Prince William is said to be 'troubled' by the prospect of a Trump visit. It's possible that he's still annoyed by Trump weighing in via Twitter about illicit photos taken of Duchess of Cambridge sunbathing *au naturel* back in 2012. (He did say she 'is great! Come on Kate!')

Prince Harry, who is quite popular in the US, was said to be devastated by Trump's election and to regard the President as a threat to human rights.

Both men are probably furious over comments Trump made about their mother, which was covered in Fact #28 and subsequent comments he made about how he could have prevented the fatal accident in Paris.

Speaker John Bercow wouldn't block a Trump visit, but also would not extend an invitation to address Parliament.

---

1 Fenton, Siobhan. 'Donald Trump and Prince Charles 'in Diplomacy Row over Climate Change' Ahead of President's First UK Visit.' *The Independent*, 29 Jan. 2017, www.independent.co.uk/news/world/americas/donald-trump-prince-charles-climate-change-environment-uk-visit-queen-a7551701.html.

Who would meet with Trump besides the Prime Minister? Jeremy Corbyn said he would be happy to take him to the Finsbury Park Mosque to teach him a little bit about diversity, according to *The Telegraph*. 'Jeremy would meet him and would like to show him different communities,' a spokesman said.[2]

London Mayor Sadiq Khan, who Trump dragged into a Twitter war after the June 2017 terrorist attacks, said in November 2017 that he does support the US-UK relationship and approves a non-state visit. 'I think it's important for the Prime Minister to have good relations with the President of the USA...there's got to be a good working relationship.' Asked if he would meet with Trump, the Mayor responded, 'I haven't been asked to meet with him, let's cross that bridge if it comes to it.'

Pressed a bit more, Khan replied that if Trump wants to meet the 'Mayor of London...I'd be happy to meet with him and show him parts of London where [citizens do] not just tolerate each other but respect, celebrate, and embrace each other. I think we can be a beacon.'[3]

So while it may not be a 'yoog' event with gilded chariots and Parliamentary honors, it will still be the best Non State Visit Ever. Believe me.

---

2 Riley-Smith, Ben. 'Donald Trump 'to Make Working Visit to Britain in Early 2018 - but He Won't Meet the Queen'.' *The Telegraph*, 11 Oct. 2017, www.telegraph.co.uk/news/2017/10/11/donald-trump-make-working-visit-britain-early-2018-without-meeting/.

3 'Sadiq Khan: I Will Meet with Donald Trump If He Comes to London.' 2 Nov. 2016, www.msn.com/en-gb/news/uknews/sadiq-khan-i-will-meet-donald-trump-when-he-comes-to-london/ar-BBESlGW.